PC User's Guide to the AS/400

PC User's Guide to the AS/400

Bradley Dyck Kliewer
Henry W. Kliewer

VNR VAN NOSTRAND REINHOLD
New York

Library of Congress Catalog Card Number 93-77963
ISBN 0-442-30878-7

I(T)P Van Nostrand Reinhold is a division of International Thomson Publishing. ITP logo is a trademark under license.

Printed in the United States of America

Van Nostrand Reinhold
115 Fifth Avenue
New York, NY 10003

International Thomson Publishing
Berkshire House
168-173 High Holborn
London WC1V 7AA, England

Thomas Nelson Australia
102 Dodds Street
South Melbourne 3205
Victoria, Australia

Nelson Canada
1120 Birchmount Road
Scarborough, Ontario MIK 5G4, Canada

16 15 14 13 12 11 10 9 8 7 6 5 4 3 2 1

Contents

Preface

The AS/400, Application Systems/400, is IBM's mid-range computer solution, designed to provide mainframe capabilities at a lower cost. Known for ease-of-use and reliability, the AS/400 is chosen by many organizations for its business applications and its database system, which provides a safe repository for corporate information resources through centralization of data.

Whatever the reasons your organization has for using the AS/400, this book provides you with an introduction to the system as well the basic tools you need to understand the AS/400 and get it up and running in your installation, whether your shop is large or small.

AUDIENCE

This book was written for system administrators, MIS heads, and other staff in MIS shops who have experience with PC-based LAN (local area network) systems. This book will help you determine whether the AS/400 is the right mid-range system for your installation's needs and will guide you through the rudiments of setting up, configuring, and administrating an AS/400 system, drawing heavily upon your PC experience. A section of the book deals specifically with PC Support, the AS/400 connectivity software that permits connection to PCs and local area networks.

Those in management may also find this book of use in the decision-making process of whether to incorporate the AS/400 into the organization's current installation or to replace the current system. The accessible style and organization of this book also will make it of use to end-users, who will be expected to come up to speed quickly on their organization's new AS/400 system.

1

Introduction

Since its introduction in 1988, the AS/400 has become one of the most popular and successful mid-range computer systems. Based on the successes of the earlier System 36 and System 38, the AS/400 has led the move to downsizing in the computing industry. The current trends of "downsizing" and "rightsizing" are rooted in the premise that the reliability, security, and processing power offered by mainframe systems are available on less costly, lower maintenance mid-range systems. This is the market niche that the AS/400 fills. The current installed base of over 200,000 AS/400s supports this theory.[1] As telling as the number of installed systems is to the success of AS/400, the size of the third party applications market is even more so. Currently, there are over 20,000 applications available from over 8,000 software vendors.[2] Third party peripherals and add-on products for the AS/400 abound. Today the AS/400 product line ranges from models equivalent to network file servers to models that rival the performance of mainframes. Initially designed as a stand-alone system, the AS/400 has found a place in the modern "enterprise computing" model that characterizes MIS shops today and is often found linked to mainframe systems, local-area networks (LANs) and even other AS/400s.

The AS/400's initial success was as a platform for downsizing. The lure of reduced costs and a simpler-to-operate system made the AS/400 attractive. This is still true today, but the rapid growth in client/server computing is providing a new role for the AS/400. Let us look at these two areas, downsizing and client/server computing, in relation to the AS/400.

DOWNSIZING

The term downsizing has numerous meanings. In the realm of information systems, it generally refers to moving applications or complete systems from large mainframe computers to smaller mini-computer systems, often at the departmental level. In recent years, downsizing has become popular due primarily to economic considerations. There are other factors in addition to economics that have made downsizing an attractive alternative, including competitive advantage, application development costs, and the emergence of departmental computing.

Competitive Advantage

Competitive advantage may be the most compelling reason to downsize. While cost is an important reason, the ability to improve an organization's competitive position may justify a downsizing move. How exactly can a downsizing solution such as the AS/400 improve a business's competitive position? The answer is that applications can generally be developed and implemented in a much shorter time frame than in a traditional mainframe environment. One study showed that 75 percent of mainframe shops had applications development backlogs of one year, and 36 percent of that number had backlogs of up to two years.[3] Delays in implementing new systems can cost not only in lost savings, but may also put the firm at a competitive disadvantage with other firms that are able to respond more quickly to changes in the marketplace. In addition, applications are generally less costly to develop on a mid-range system in comparison to a mainframe environment. The availability of packaged software solutions may in some cases eliminate the need for costly custom programming. If programming is required, the availability of application development tools such as fourth generation languages, relational databases, and computer-aided software engineering (CASE) tools make the AS/400 an attractive application development environment.

Application Development Costs

As previously mentioned, application development costs are generally less on mid-range systems in comparison to mainframes. This is in some part due to the availability of packaged software solutions that are often implemented "right out of the box" and require no custom programming. The AS/400 architecture offers application developers a "technology-independent" platform because the hardware and operating system can be replace or upgraded with no impact on the application programs.[4] While the majority of application development is still done by in-house staff, the trend among AS/400 users appears to be toward the use of more packaged software applications. A recent survey revealed that 36 percent of AS/400 applications were packaged solutions, 53 percent were developed by in-house staff, and the remaining 11 percent were developed by outside sources.[5] If application development is required, the AS/400 offers an integrated database as well as supports many popular fourth generation languages such as FOCUS from Information Builders and PROGRESS from Progress Software. Another advantage is that the AS/400 offers the ability to integrate applications both on the AS/400 and on connected platforms such as local-area networks. Many vendors of products for the PC/LAN market have compatible products for the AS/400 that can easily integrate applications and data from the two platforms. When downsizing from a mainframe platform, there may be situations where packaged software cannot meet the business needs of the organizations. In this situation, it is often preferable to move the existing mainframe application to the AS/400 rather than develop a new application. While this may seem like a formidable task, there are software packages available to support the migration of applications from the mainframe to the AS/400. The functionality of the mainframe application can be realized on the AS/400 without the need to rewrite the existing application.

Departmental Computing

A recent trend in the computing industry is departmental computing. In the early days of the information age, all data processing functions were highly centralized and individual departments or divisions in an organization had little involvement in the IS department other than as end users of a service. As mid-range systems such as the AS/400 began to appear on the market, these new platforms were installed in the user departments rather than in the centralized IS departments. Departments began to find that they were better able to respond to the unique needs of their department with their own processing capabilities. Often with a centralized IS department there were long application development backlogs, and the question of priorities was difficult to resolve. Which application should take priority in the development queue? The new application for finance or the new marketing application? Departmental computing systems allowed individual business units to prioritize their information needs and reallocate resources as needed.

While departmental computing does have advantages, it also has disadvantages. With independence comes incompatibility. As individual departments pursue their own directions and develop their own applications, the overall enterprise may be fragmenting into small "islands of information." An application in a manufacturing division may contain information that is needed by other divisions such as finance or marketing. The concept of enterprise computing attempts to tie together all the automated systems in an organization and present them a single source accessible by anyone in the organization. The AS/400 offers some advantages in this type of situation with its homogeneous operating system and database. Additionally, the advanced peer-to-peer networking (APPN) and advanced program-to-program communications (APPC) features of the AS/400 support the linking of multiple systems and applications.

Economics

While perhaps the most visible advantage of downsizing, cost savings are often a secondary benefit to some of the previously mentioned reasons for downsizing. Cost savings can be realized in a number of areas. Most notable are hardware costs. AS/400 systems range from a list price of just over $10,000 for low-end models to over $1,000,000 for the high-end systems.[6] In relation to the price of a mainframe system, this is a considerable savings. Additionally, the environmental support requirements of the AS/400 are generally less than those of a mainframe and result in lower facilities cost. In some situations, AS/400s have literally been installed in closets and under desktops. In terms of software, the cost of packaged AS/400 applications is approaching the cost of PC LAN software. For example, accounting packages run from $750 and up.[7] Complete turnkey systems for business and governmental applications that include hardware and software are available for a fraction of the cost of a comparable mainframe solution. Ongoing support requirements for the AS/400 are much lower as well. Often hardware support is handled by maintenance support agreements. Many of the components in the AS/400 are rack mounted and are easily replaced if needed. If packaged software solutions are used, software support would most likely consist of applying upgrades and new releases. Often the tasks can be performed by a systems administrator, so the need and cost of in-house programming support is eliminated. In many installations, the AS/400 is supported by a single systems administrator responsible for hardware support, software support, and systems administration. Hardware upgrades and the addition of new peripherals are greatly simplified by the modular rack mounted design of the AS/400. In most situations, the new hardware components are added to the existing equipment. This eliminates the need and cost of replacing the entire system or portions of it in order to add additional capabilities.

DOWNSIZING AND THE AS/400

The AS/400 is in the forefront of the downsizing movement. Specifically, the AS/400 supports downsizing strategy by:

- Improving the competitive position of the business unit by providing a more flexible and responsive information system
- Reducing the application development cycle and providing business solutions quicker
- Reducing overall computing costs

In addition to downsizing, upsizing also accounts for a significant share of the AS/400 market. Many of the AS/400 upsizing customers are System 36 and System 38 users who are moving to the AS/400 for increased performance. One survey showed that over half of AS/400 sales were from System 36/38 migration.[8]

CLIENT/SERVER COMPUTING

Client/server computing has recently become one of the most talked about topics in the computing industry. The goal of client/server computing is to split up the computing process and place elements of it on the platforms best suited for a particular task. For example, PCs and workstations are good at presenting information to users via a graphical user interface. Mainframe or midrange systems such as the AS/400 are good at storing and retrieving data. Client/server computing seeks to maximize the relative advantages of each type of platform. A program running on a PC would take a request from a user via a graphical user interface. In processing the request, the PC application may then request certain data from a database server located on an AS/400. An application or database management system running on the AS/400 would then search the database and return only those records meeting the criteria specified by the PC application. The request may be for all sales data for the month of July. After retrieving the information, the application or database management system would then send the information back to the PC client. The PC client would then present the data to the user, perhaps graphically in the form of a chart or graph. Figure 1.1 illustrates this type of configuration.

The AS/400 is well suited to this type of role because of its widespread use, integrated database, and communications capabilities. The security and data integrity found in mainframe environments are replicated in the AS/400. Developments in several technologies have contributed to the growth of client/server

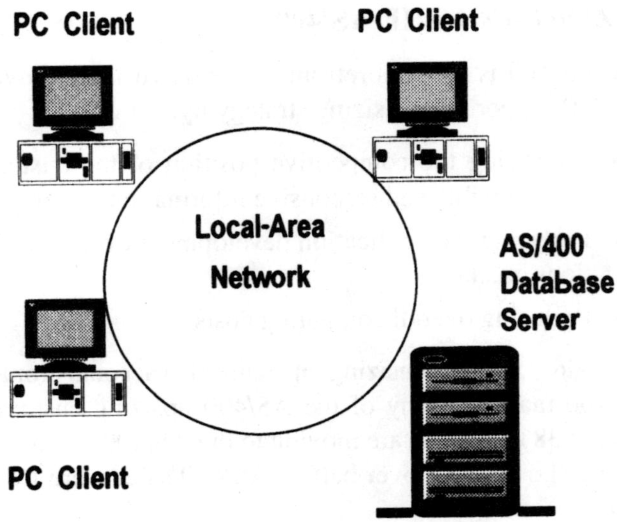

Figure 1.1 Client/server configuration

computing. Four major technologies are personal computers and workstations, data communications, database management software, and graphical user interfaces.

Personal Computers and Workstations

Advances in personal computers and workstations have dramatically increased the processing power available on the desktop. Client/server computing depends on this newfound desktop computing power to run graphical user interfaces and client applications. While compute power has increased, costs have dramatically decreased. PCs and workstations offer a low cost method to increase processing capability without upgrading or replacing a central host. Many of the "dumb" terminals attached to AS/400s and mainframes have now been replaced with powerful PCs. These PCs can then be used to access and manipulate the vast amounts of data stored on the host systems. Many third party vendors offer PC-to-AS/400 connectivity products. As more and more RISC-based workstations appear on the market, it can be expected that they too will become clients for AS/400 database servers.

Data Communications

Data communications technology servers as the "glue" that connects together the many pieces of a modern enterprise network. This may take the form of a local-area network (LAN) or a even a wide-area network (WAN). In AS/400 installations, the use of LANs as a means to communicate between a PC and the AS/400 is becoming more common. A recent survey has reported that 77 percent of large AS/400 sites had installed LANs.[9] IBM's advanced peer-to-peer networking provides the AS/400 with the capability to communicate with other platforms on a peer-to-peer basis. Often AS/400s are connected to other AS/400s or mainframes via an APPN network. Why is peer-to-peer communication important? Under IBM's System Network Architecture or SNA, networks were hierarchical and a central communications controller managed all communications with attached devices. Figure 1.2 shows a typical SNA environment and its hierarchical arrangement of communications devices. Communications are basically in one direction, from the host to the attached device. The device simply displays the information provided by the host and accepts input for the host.

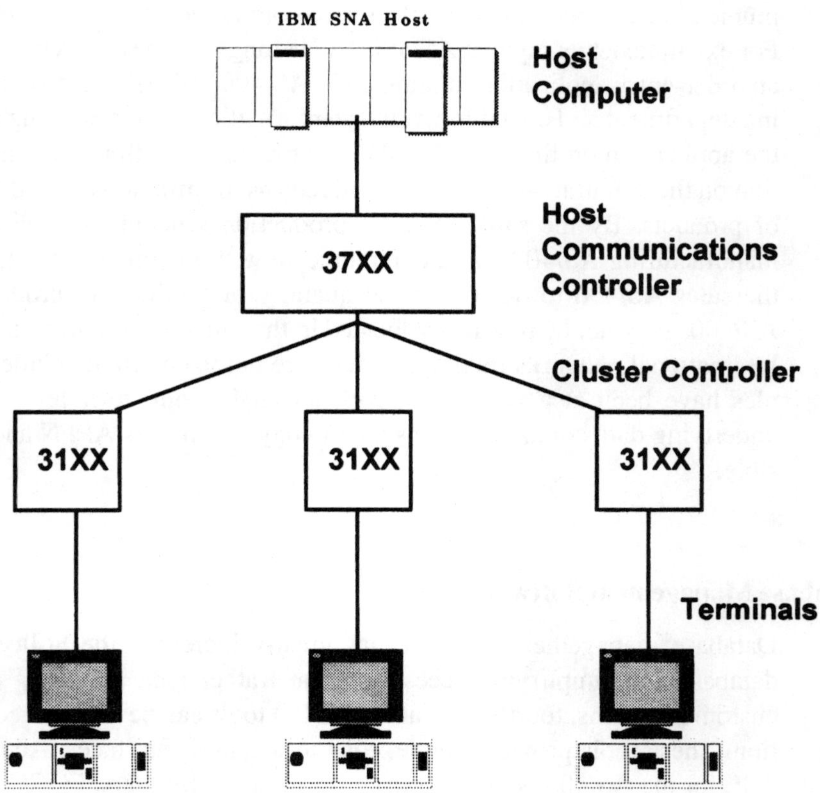

Figure 1.2 A typical SNA environment

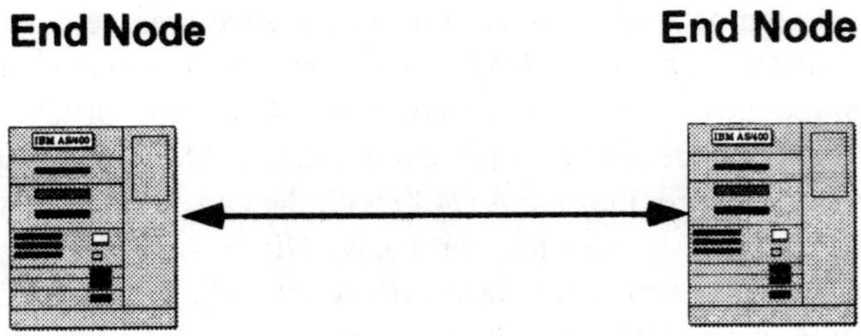

Figure 1.3 A typical APPN

Under APPN each device in the network controls its communications with the other devices on the network. Figure 1.3 shows a typical APPN network. Each AS/400 is configured as an "end node" and may initiate communications with the other host. Neither host controls the communications network, but rather they interact as peers, establishing and breaking communications links as needed.

Through APPN, applications can utilize advanced program-to-program communications, which allows platforms to communicate at an applications level. For example, let us say that AS/400 "A" belongs to the sales department and has an order-entry application running on it. AS/400 "B" belongs to the manufacturing department and contains inventory information. When entering a sales order, the application on the sales AS/400 communicates with the inventory application on the manufacturing AS/400 and returns information about the availability of products. By the same token, a production scheduling application on the manufacturing AS/400 could communicate with the order entry application on the sales AS/400 to determine the quantity of products to produce. The two AS/400s may not be physically located in the same plant or even the same state. International networks linking AS/400s are not uncommon. While these examples have been at a very high level, the main point to note is that it is the underlying data communications technology that makes APPN and APPC possible.

Database Management Software

Database management software has greatly increased the utility of business databases by simplifying access to data. Rather than accessing data through custom programs, fourth generation (4GLs) tools can be used to access information. These tools provide simple, easy-to-use user interfaces. An example of a 4GL for the AS/400 is FOCUS from Information Builders. FOCUS provides an end user ad-hoc reporting tool to access data on the AS/400. Through the use of

Structured Query Language or SQL, applications programs can be written to run on client platforms that access AS/400 database servers. The advantage to using SQL is that only the requested data is returned to the client application rather than the entire database. This minimizes network traffic and reduces the amount of data that the client application must process. Additionally, SQL allows the use of many 4GL report writers and application development packages and provides a "generic" means to access data. This eliminates the need for the end user or applications developer to have a detailed understanding of the underlying database management system.

Graphical User Interfaces

As software has become advanced, it has also become more difficult to use. Usually there was little commonality between applications and much time was spent training users. Graphical user interfaces help to provide commonality across applications and make application usage more intuitive. A picture of a stop sign is easier to comprehend as the way to stop a program than is a specific function key. Not only is program control simpler to understand, so is the information presented by the application. A spreadsheet of values may provide the required information, but a color graph of the data may convey more meaning to the user. The two most popular graphical user interfaces are Microsoft Windows and IBM's OS/2 Presentation Manager. Both have the ability to interface with the AS/400 and have graphical development packages available. Using these graphical development tools, complete applications can be built without coding. Data on the AS/400 can be retrieved and graphically displayed for end users.

CLIENT/SERVER AND THE AS/400

All of the above technologies have contributed to the development of client/server computing. The AS/400 is in a position to support client/server computing because of:

- Its ability to communicate to PCs and workstations via LANs and terminal emulation
- The ability of the AS/400 to utilize advance peer-to-peer communication (APPN) and advanced program-to-program communications (APPC)
- The integrated AS/400 database and the ability to run popular industry standard relational databases that support SQL

- The development of graphical interfaces and application development tools for the AS/400

The AS/400's role in client/server computing is underscored by IBM's introduction of a suite of client/server products for end users and application developers. The AS/400 has and will continue to serve as a database servers for PC and LAN client/server applications. In addition to client/server software, two new AS/400 models were recently introduced that are designed specifically as LAN database servers.[10]

SUMMARY

This text is designed to help AS/400 users and system administrators set up and use a basic AS/400. It would be particularly useful for installations that are setting up a turnkey system and have no prior AS/400 experience. While a complete course in AS/400 system administration is beyond the scope of this book, the major tasks of system administration, operation, and configuration are presented in sufficient detail to provide a basic level of familiarity with the AS/400. Chapter two introduces the basic concepts of system administration and system security along with a brief introduction to AS/400 system configuration. Chapter 3 discusses AS/400 connectivity and goes into detail about installing the PC Support communications package on DOS and OS/2 workstations. Chapter 4 covers the AS/400 system architecture and explains the file structure and database system. Information on database design creation and manipulation is presented. Chapter 5 introduces Control Language Programming and the automation of system functions. Chapter 6 discusses the object-oriented design tools available on the AS/400 and presents an example of how an application could be developed using them. Chapter 7 discusses the use of high-level languages such as RPG and C on the AS/400. Chapter 8 goes into detail on the AS/400 security system and its administration. Chapter 9 introduces the concept of work management and resource allocation and how they can be used to control the flow of work through the AS/400. Appendix A provides useful information for users of PC Support who wish to configure HP Laserjet printer as system printers. Appendix B covers automatic configuration. It is assumed that the reader has some basic understanding of the AS/400 and PC workstations. Additional information on the topics covered in the text can be found in the IBM AS/400 system documentation.

REFERENCES

1. "Answering Corporate Needs with Client/Server Computing," Supplement to *Datamation*, June 15, 1993, p. S-12.
2. "Meeting IS Integration Needs with the AS/400," Supplement to *Datamation*, August 15, 1993, p. S-25.
3. Dwight B. Davis, "Building Up Steam for '93," *Datamation*, June 1, 1992, p. 51.
4. "Meeting IS Integration Needs with the AS/400," op. cit., p. S-5.
5. "Meeting IS Integration Needs with the AS/400," op. cit., p. S-10.
6. *IBM AS/400 System Additions*, International Business Machines Corporation, 1993, p. 12.
7. *AS/400 Catalog Summer 1993*, International Business Machines Corporation, 1993, p. 37.
8. Robert Moran, "Deconstructing the AS/400," *Information Week*, August 23, 1993, p. 18.
9. "Meeting IS Integration Needs with the AS/400," op. cit., p. S-4.
10. *IBM AS/400 System Additions*, op. cit., p. 13.

2

Using the AS/400

Before you even begin to install an AS/400, you should understand some of the basic user functions assigned in a secure system. For the examples in this book, it will be assumed that you are working in a small shop and will be in charge of the AS/400 system. If you are working in a larger company that already has an AS/400 installed, you may not have access to all of the facilities mentioned here. Even if you cannot access all of the maintenance functions, you should find it helpful to know what is happening behind the scenes—and why the MIS people may be grumbling about some of the strange things the PC users are doing to the system. You owe it to yourself, and your MIS staff, to make your operations run as smoothly as possible.

ACCESS LEVELS

There are five basic levels of access to an AS/400. These functions are generally called the Security Officer, the Security Administrator, the System Operator, the Programmer, and (at the low rung of the ladder) the User. Should the need arise, it is possible to mix and match features of the various access levels. Each level is assigned a default name that can be used as a *profile* to create new user names with the same access rights.

Security Officer

The Security Officer has full system access. The Security Officer can change passwords, set access authority to files and programs, change system configurations, and generally do whatever he or she wants to do on the system. In most companies, the real Security Officer (profile QSECOFR) never logs on. The password is locked away in a safe, and another ID is set to a similarly high privilege. However, the access is an enhanced Security Administrator (see the next description) rather than a full Security Officer.

Such measures can help avert total disaster should a disgruntled (and soon to be ex-) Security Officer attempt to sabotage the system. If you have not installed security options on your system, any knowledgeable user will have access to the Security Officer profile. This is not generally a good idea, except maybe in a lab setting where another, more secure system does the real work.

Security Administrator

The Security Administrator (profile QSECADM) has more restricted access than the Security Officer. Of particular note, the Security Administrator cannot access or change rights to an individual's or department's private files, although there are other access restrictions, too. The Security Administrator's primary task is creating new user profiles to add users to the system.

System Operator

The System Operator (profile QSYSOPR) handles the maintenance chores on a system. In a large operation (with a system that runs 24 hours a day) there will always be System Operators on duty, working in shifts. These people make sure that the printers are well supplied and operating smoothly, keep the terminals and PCs properly connected to the system, manage the system backup, and perform other similar duties.

Programmers

Programmers (profile QPGMR) traditionally have fairly unrestrained access to a system. As an example, a programmer in the default setup may perform the PWRDWNSYS command; that stands for "power down system" and is essentially the same as hitting an off switch (of course, the name of any user who activates such a command appears in the history log, so anyone who would do something so drastic without good reason could certainly expect a stern warning from the Security Officer, if not worse). Programmers need a high level of access to create and test their programs. However, like the Security Officer, the access rights are often restricted a bit beyond the system defaults.

Users

Users (profile QUSER) have very restricted access. In many installations, they are further restricted to the menus that are available—the command line prompts you will be using in this chapter would not even be available. This setting was designed for the novice user who needs only a few functions to perform his or her job.

PC SUPPORT

Because you will be making extensive use of PCs connected to the AS/400, PC Support will be one of your core applications. PC Support is sold as a single software package, but it is really several different programs under one name. PC Support includes two core packages: Terminal emulation (called the Workstation Function) and a file serving product akin to a network file server (the Folder Function).

These functions are more clearly delineated under OS/2. OS/2 supports the terminal emulation through Extended Services (also called Communications Manager). The OS/2 version of PC Support handles the file serving and data transfer operations. However, you must establish a Communications Manager connection before PC Support will work (in addition to the terminal emulation, Communications Manager also provides the APPN (advanced peer-to-peer networking) connections required by PC Support).

It is perhaps tempting to compare PC Support to a standard local-area network (LAN) program. Like a LAN, PC Support can be connected through several different media types: Token Ring, Ethernet, RS-232 (ASCII), and Twinax. The latter two types are considered the economy routes since they connect via the AS/400's standard workstation connectors.

HARDWARE CONNECTIONS

Twinax is IBM's standard AS/400 terminal configuration. If your site already has an AS/400 installed, it probably uses Twinax connections. The PC must have a Twinax-compatible adapter (usually a 5250 emulator board) installed to connect to the AS/400. Twinax is fast and simple to install and use. However, it is fairly expensive compared to ASCII. Almost every item involved in a Twinax installation costs more: Cabling, terminals, modems, and adapter boards for the PCs.

If you are upgrading a predominantly new PC site to an AS/400 installation, you should consider installing an ASCII workstation controller on the AS/400 rather than the Twinax controller. With the ASCII controller, you can connect your PCs through the RS-232 serial port—standard equipment on most PCs manufactured today. The disadvantage of the ASCII controller is the limited data throughput for file transfer tasks. On the other hand, if most of your PCs are not on the same site as the AS/400 and you need to connect to several outside telephone lines, the AS/400 ASCII controller can work with standard Hayes-compatible modems. Most PC-oriented businesses would find ASCII communications to be the most economical route.

Assuming you want better throughput than ASCII provides and you are willing to pay a premium, you should consider installing a network adapter on the AS/400 in addition to an ASCII workstation controller. The ASCII workstation controller will give you economical RS-232 connections for simple workstations or outside lines, and the network adapter will give you the performance advantage you need for more data-intensive tasks, such as file transfers.

Note that whatever cabling method you choose, PC Support can implement all of its functions over the same line. For example, both terminal emulation and data transfer can use a Token Ring network for communications. As of this writing, however, OS/2 PC Support does not work on an RS-232 connection, since Communications Manager cannot establish APPN connections over RS-232.

LEARNING THE OPERATING SYSTEM

Before you actually begin setting up connections (other than the initial console), you should learn some of the more important system maintenance tasks. System setup is fairly automatic (as long as you do not tell the system to disable automatic configuration). However, you may occasionally run into some problems. If you already know some basic tasks, such as managing printer output and changing configuration options, you will be better able to cope with any problems that occur. When you hear people talk about the AS/400, several terms will occur with great frequency: Queues, jobs, libraries, and files. Some of these terms can be a bit disconcerting to PC users because the concepts do not always match the same terminology as used on the PC. Take queues, for example. On the PC, most people would associate a queue with the printer, calling the buffered output either a print queue or a print spooler. On the AS/400, this is called an *output queue*, and it is only one of several different types of queues including job and message queues, among others.

All of these queues share a common feature: They hold a list of operations waiting for a triggering event. A job queue holds a list of jobs (akin to batch files on a PC) that are waiting to process. The message queue holds messages from the system to one or more of the users on the system. For a PC user, this feature takes some getting used to. When you run a program such as a compiler on a PC, the system writes the error messages to the screen as they occur. On the AS/400, however, many of these messages are sent to a queue to await a view command from the user (who may be busy doing something else when the error occurs), just as an output queue stores printed output until a printer is free to print the report. This, then, is one of the first tasks that you should learn to manage—reading the messages that the system sends to your queue. The system does at least have the courtesy to notify you when an important, unread message is in the queue (the severity level at which this happens is adjustable through the CHGMSGQ command). These messages are called *notify* messages. When you receive a notify message, a "Message Waiting" indicator at the bottom of the screen is turned on. Depending on your terminal type, this may appear as a highlighted "MW" or a page icon (5250 terminals) or a mark along the rightmost column (ASCII terminals). If the message is particularly severe, the system may send a *break* message, which interrupts your work and displays the message immediately. You may also specify whether all messages meeting the severity level should be delivered as break messages.

Queued Messages

As with most tasks on the AS/400, there are several ways to retrieve messages. The most straightforward is to type "DSPMSG" at a command line. The system will then display messages in your default message queue. Note that it is the default queue that displays. Potentially, you could have messages waiting in several different queues. A more adaptable command in this case is WRKMSGQ *ALL, which will display a list of queues. You may then select a queue (or several queues) to display from the list.

Commands are also available through the system menus. You will find the message handling selections under the "General System Tasks" menu (option 3). From there, select the "Messages" menu (option 4), and finally either "Display Messages" (option 3) or "Work with Message Queues" (option 6).

However, when you use the menu something happens a bit differently; you end up at a prompt screen. For example, the "Display Messages" option prompts for a message queue name (and optionally, the library name and output destination). Some of the parameter lines already contain entries; these are the defaults that were used when you used DSPMSG from the command line. You can either hit enter to accept the defaults or change them as desired. In this case, you would simply hit enter to accept *WRKUSR, a reserved name that selects messages both from the workstation's queue (messages about the physical connection) and the user profile queue (messages for the user who is currently logged on). Most messages will be sent to the user profile queue.

At this point, you might realize that you can alter the command operation by typing parameters directly on the command line:

```
DSPMSG   *WRKUSR    Display workstation and user messages
DSPMSG   *WRKSTN    Display workstation messages
DSPMSG   *USRPRF    Display user messages
DSPMSG   BKLIEWER   Display messages for queue BKLIEWER
```

Prompt Mode

That is fine if you can remember the parameters, but are you stuck with the menu system if you don't remember? No. After typing a command on the command line, you can hit the prompt key (F4) to go directly to the prompt screen (do not pass through menus, do not collect unnecessary keystrokes).

Selecting Parameters

Now, if you are really adventuresome, you have a few more interesting function keys available from the prompt screen. The prompt screen presents the most fundamental options in a concise format. It is sufficient for 90 percent of the work you will be doing. However, most AS/400 commands have a plethora of options that you may seldom see or use. You can see these additional options by hitting the all parameters key (F9). Now you will see that DSPMSG will optionally let you select a message type, the message order, the minimum severity code to display, and an assistance level. If you want to learn more about these parameters, you can move to one of the prompt lines and hit the help key (F1).

The AS/400 user interface can prompt you, it can help you. But wait, there is more! The AS/400 Control Language can get unwieldy; if you need a reminder of that, just look at that long row of shelf space used by the Control Language manuals. Remembering the position of every parameter could be a daunting memorization task. In fact, the AS/400 limits the number of positional parameters for each command. Instead, each parameter has an associated keyword. From the prompt menu, you can see the keywords by hitting the keywords key (F11). By using keywords, the parameter order becomes irrelevant (the DSPMSG command allows only one positional parameter—the queue name.)

Command Line Parameters

Now, you can enter a command that skips several parameters:

```
DSPMSG BKLIEWER SEV(30) OUTPUT(*PRINT)
```

or

```
DSPMSG OUTPUT(*PRINT) SEV(30) MSGQ(BKLIEWER)
```

either of which will send all level 30 messages and above from the BKLIEWER message queue to the printer. If you mix positional and keyword parameters as in the first example, the positional parameters must be listed first.

This may all seem somewhat strange, but it is similar to many of the conventions used from the DOS command line. For example, a DOS command can have required parameters along with "switches" that are positionally independent. A DOS command might use notation such as:

```
FORMAT A: /F:720
```

Caution! Where DOS generally uses a slash or dash followed by a letter and a colon (or equal sign), the AS/400 uses a keyword and parentheses. Watch out for the position-sensitive keywords, however! With DOS, you can generally place position-sensitive data either before or after the switches; on the AS/400, the position-sensitive data must always come first.

As you begin working with the AS/400, you will probably experience some frustration as you learn the new commands and architecture. If you cannot remember a command, try navigating the menus, but as you become more experienced, wean yourself away from the menu system. Command lines are available from many AS/400 screens, and typing a direct command from one of these screens is much more efficient than backing out of the current menu and then up through the desired menu.

In the beginning, as you work through the menu screens, you will sometimes see a command in parentheses following the menu title:

```
Display Messages (DSPMSG)
```

This is the command that will bring you directly to the screen. In this way, you can use the menus to learn the commands.

IBM also designed a consistent naming convention that should help you learn the commands. For example, display commands begin with DSP and work with commands begin with WRK. Most commands are grouped into three-letter abbreviations, although there are a some exceptions, such as WRKDEVD for work with device descriptions and WRKMSGQ, which you have already seen.

WORKING WITH PRINTERS

You may have noticed that the last few command examples redirected output to a printer. Much of your initial work on the AS/400 will probably be spent setting up the printers. There are two key properties of AS/400 printers that you must remember. First, many printers may be connected to an AS/400. In a large organization, each department may have a printer or two in a handy location, so the AS/400 must have a way to associate each user (or each terminal) with a particular printer. After all, you would not want to run all the way to the other end of the building to retrieve the output when there is a printer sitting right next to you.

There are many ways to associate a printer with the current output: By workstation location, user name, the particular program controlling the output, etc. Most of the time, you will associate a printer with the location of the workstation. Then, if a user moves from a terminal in an office at one end of the building to a terminal in the computer room at the other end of the building, the nearest printer in the computer room will be used. Had the printer been associated with the user, the printer at the office would have been used, making for a long walk from the computer room to the office (and a very disgruntled user). When security is a concern, such as accounting data, or a particular print quality is required, such as laser printer output of word processing documents, you might assign the printer to a specific user or application. For now, you should learn how to select a default printer, manage the print queue, and alter report formats.

Setting the Default Queue

Although it is not required, if you install a printer on the system console, you will find it is very useful for problem determination and resolution. The AS/400 assumes that you will be using wide (132-column) printers for most system output. If you use the first workstation attachment, a very dumb, very cheap parallel printer will work well. In fact, it can be difficult to configure any attributes (such as compressed printer or near-letter quality) for the console printer. The AS/400 configures the first workstation attachment's printer as a model 5256—a simple 10-CPI, 132-column printer. You can use a narrow

(80-column printer) for the default system printer, but you must have a way to get it into 132-column mode (compressed print).

On the first workstation attachment, you can use the terminal setup printer to select the appropriate printer model. The AS/400 will then automatically reset the printer to compressed print when appropriate. But, if you have an unsupported 80-column printer, you will need to set compressed mode manually every once in a while. This is not a frequent occurrence (e.g., when the system is booted—IPL in IBM's lingo), but it can be rather annoying.

There is a fairly common problem with this setup in a microcomputer environment. Most PC printers are 80 column in the default font. As you get proficient with the system, you will want to send system reports to the workstation you are currently using, rather than the system console. You can get 132 columns on your PC printers, but the AS/400 must signal the printer to change fonts. Of course, you can tell the AS/400 to use compressed print for its reports, but then the AS/400 will send an error message to the System Operator each time you send a report with compressed attributes to the console. Why? Because the AS/400 thinks the console printer is a dumb, 10-CPI, 132-column printer; it cannot switch the printer to compressed mode, so the system sends a message to the System Operator. The System Operator must reply to the message before the system will print the job.

The AS/400 does not understand printer widths very well. Indeed, the system will merrily send a 132-column report to a 10-CPI, 80-column printer with nary a suspicion that something is wrong. It does, however, understand font attributes and will complain vociferously if something seems amiss. Of course, you know that your console printer is really using compressed print and will handle the output just fine, and the System Operator can tell the AS/400 to either cancel the job, go ahead and process the job, or hold the job for later processing. If you select "G," the AS/400 will print the job, and if the printer is already set for compressed printing, all will be well.

However, the AS/400 will prompt for the CPI settings every time a new job comes across. Wouldn't it be nice to automate the replies? That is precisely what you can do with something called a *reply list*. Access to such system resources in a secure system typically requires security administrator authority (e.g., QSECOFR or the equivalent). Unless you have such access rights, you cannot perform many of the operations outlined in the following sections. If you are in charge of installing and/or configuring a new AS/400 for your office, you should have the appropriate access rights.

If you are accessing an established corporate AS/400, it would be unreasonable to expect the MIS department to grant you the necessary rights for many of the following tasks. Many of these commands could have undesirable side effects in a large installation not oriented toward PC users. You should still study these sections so that you understand the issues involved, and then you can work with the MIS department to help lessen the demands and problems your department may add to the MIS department's administration tasks.

No matter what your access rights, you should be able to view the reply list. If you log on as the Security Officer, however, you will also have sufficient rights to change the reply list. In either case, enter the WRKRPYLE command (work with reply list entries). You will then see a list of sequence numbers, message IDs, replies, and compare values. The sequence number simply tells the system what order to use when looking up relies. When the system sends a message that needs a reply, it first looks at the reply list.

Starting with the lowest sequence number, the system compares the error message ID to the message ID in the reply list. In the simplest case, if all three letters and four digits match, the listed reply is sent to the system, and the System Operator does not need to intervene. Suppose you look at the font ID message you see that the error number was CPA3361. To continue, you type "G." If you have sufficient access rights, you can add message ID CPA3361 with a reply of "G" if you never want the System Operator to be prompted for a font mismatch. To do this, hit the add (F6) key and enter the relevant data: a sequence number (any number not currently used), a message identifier (CPA3361), and a message reply (G). You may leave the comparison data and message data start position set to *NONE. When you return to the reply list display, hit the refresh key (F5) to see the new entry.

If you come from a PC background, prompting for mismatched CPI settings may seem rather strange. After all, on a PC most printers have many different font sizes available, and if you set something wrong, you simply expect misaligned output. Printers for minicomputers and mainframes have long been of a different breed. Because they are designed for long print jobs accessed by perhaps hundreds of users, these printers are often designed more for speed and durability than convenience. One type, called a band printer, has a long, heavy band that is used to form the characters. It is limited to a single character size, but you can change bands if another size is needed.

Of course changing a band is not a quick, simple operation. Thus, the AS/400 was designed to alert the System Operator whenever a change is required. The System Operator can then decide whether to change the band, send the output to another printer that is properly configured, or hold the file and print it later when the band can be changed (perhaps when several print files have queued up that require the same band). So, you may not want to totally ignore a CPI change, particularly if you have a larger installation with dedicated AS/400 printers.

Fortunately, you can add further restrictions to the reply list processing; that is what the compare value and compare start parameters are for. You can tell the system to search for a particular value in the message (e.g., the name of the printer) and only apply the reply if that value is found. The details of this operation are beyond the scope of this book; however, if you are working with an established system, the MIS department will probably use the compare values to restrict the automatic reply to the PC printers.

Not only can you narrow the scope of the search, but you may also widen the scope. For example, suppose the default reply list entries have message IDs ending with one or more 0s. Actual message IDs do not end in 0s, so the trailing 0s act as place holders. The 0s mean any message in this family (e.g., CPA0700 to CPA0799) should use the designated reply. This is where the sequence number comes into play; to generate exceptions to the general processing, the specific message ID should have a lower sequence number than the general message ID from the same family (e.g., CPA3361 should have a lower sequence number than CPA3000).

You may want to add similar reply list entries to automatically handle form changes and initial alignment. In a large environment where forms run in batches (check printing, invoices, purchase orders, etc.) it is nice to have a system that notifies the operator when a paper change is required. However, in a smaller office, where plain paper output is used, or even in a larger installation where certain printers are dedicated to a form type, the prompting can become annoying. Fortunately, alignment prompts and form prompts are not as common (e.g., occurring after the system reboots or a printer is disabled and then re-enabled).

Altering Report Formats

Okay, so here you are. You have worked through a fairly long discourse on printer attributes and CPI settings, but you have not yet seen the console printer acting strangely. It has either been printing in compressed mode the whole time or working merrily away at 10 CPI on a wide printer. What is there to worry about? Plenty, if you have not yet tried to use a printer attached to your PC.

IBM can keep fairly tight control over the printers that attach directly to the AS/400. Because both the computer and the printers were designed in-house, you can expect fairly smooth coordination between them. On the other hand, IBM has little control over the types of printers attached to a PC, and hence the support for a PC printer may or may not behave as well as you would like. On the one hand, many dot matrix printers (including IBM's Proprinters and the Lexmark PPS series) are based on the Epson command set. The closer a printer resembles the Proprinter variations of the Epson commands, the better it will work with PC Support. On the other hand, newer printer technologies typically use Postscript or a variation of Hewlett-Packard's PCL (the control language used on the LaserJet printers).

While some of these printer command sets are supported by PC Support, they are often not as refined as the IBM printer drivers. For example, as of this writing, HP LaserJet support was included. However, the AS/400 continually prompted the Security Officer for font changes and when a page was sent to the printer, it would go off-line and the printer's control panel would signal manual paper feed. Fortunately, you can customize the printer descriptions for PC Support. If you have a totally unsupported printer, or even if you just want to make your printer work more elegantly, you can create your own printer function tables. Sample reconfiguration instructions for the HP LaserJet appear in Appendix A.

Once you have your printers set up to select (or ignore) compressed print, you can start changing the report formats. Although it is possible to change all of the system reports in one fell swoop, you should probably work with one or two reports until the settings work with all or most of your printers.

Changing Report Formats

Of course, before your reports will start printing in a convenient compressed typeface on your PC printer, you must tell the AS/400 to use a compressed typeface. Before you begin changing all of the system reports to compressed print, you should test the settings on a single report. To find a convenient test report, you should first send a report to the printer and then make a note of its name.

It would be rather inconvenient to send the report and then jump over to the output queue to see the file name before it prints. In order to work at a more leisurely pace, you can first tell the output queue to delay printing the reports until further notice. To do this, enter WRKOUTQ (work with output queue), move to the name of the printer you are using (e.g., HPLJ_II_1), and select option 3 (Hold).

Now you can move to the command line and print one of the files whose format you want to change; for example, DSPMSG OUTPUT(*PRINT). To see the report name, move back to the printer and select option 5 (Work With). The name of the report file appears under the file column. For DSPMSG, the report file is QPDSPMSG.

The CHGPRTF command is used to change the printer file; in this case, CHGPRTF QPDSPMSG. The print attributes (such as characters per inch) are part of the CHGPRTF command, so you should use the F4 key, rather than

Enter, to display the available parameters. Change the CPI setting to a compressed setting, such as 15, and hit Enter. The file waiting in the output queue will not be affected, but every new print job using that report will use compressed print.

Of course, you have only changed one file of many. The QSYS library (where QPDSPMSG resides) has well over 100 different print files. Most of these are 132 columns. If you want to change all of them at once, you can use CHGPRTF QSYS/*ALL. When you hit F4, note the difference in the screen appearance as compared to CHGPRTF QPDSPMSG. In the latter case, the parameters were filled with the current values. When you select *ALL print files the system cannot display current values; obviously every report could have a unique combination of attributes. Instead, the special value *SAME is placed by each parameter. This tells the system to leave the parameter unchanged. By replacing *SAME with a specific value, such as 15 for CPI, all the reports will be changed to compressed print without affecting the other parameters.

You may find some files (such as QPDCCTL) that print correctly at 10 CPI, but there are relatively few such files, and it would be simpler to change them back to 10 CPI as you find them, rather than individully change the other reports from 10 to 15 CPI. Furthermore, it is much easier to read an 80-column report (at 15 CPI) printed on a 132-column page, than a 132-column report printed on an 80-column page!

Managing the Print Queue

You may have noticed a few references to the print queue in the previous sections. You have selected a printer from the output queue (through the WRKOUTQ) and told it to hold the reports until further notice (option 3). Indeed, if you have performed the preceding tasks, you may have one or more reports stuck waiting in the print queue. You can release them with option 6.

At the main level (work with all output queues), hold and release control every print job in the queue. There may be times when you want to hold a single job. In this case, you can take option 5 (work with) to see a list of the spooled report files. This level (work with output queue) lets you hold (option 3) and release (option 6) a single report. You may also select option 4 to delete a report—a very handy option if you accidentally send a wrong report of several hundred pages to the printer.

There is yet a faster and more convenient way to get to a single report when something has gone awry. The WRKSPLF command will list all of the print jobs you have sent. It will also list multiple queues—quite handy if the output ends up at an unexpected printer. The option numbering for hold, delete, and release is the same through the WRKOUTQ method. As you work with the AS/400, you will discover a consistency among the function key and option numbering conventions that make the system easier to learn.

You should practice holding and releasing print jobs at both the queue and individual report levels. Then, if you get into a tricky situation, you will not need to scramble for the manuals in order to bring a wild print job under control.

SUMMARY

A secure AS/400 system defines five basic access levels (user profiles) for accessing the system:

1. QSECOFR—Security Officer: Manages users and configures system settings
2. QSECADM—Security Adminstrator: Creates user profiles
3, QSYSOPR—System Operator: Manages system resources
4. QPGMR—Programmer: Writes programs and works with batch jobs
5. QUSER—User: Runs applications

You have had a brief introduction to the AS/400 hardware and terminal connections. In a PC-oriented business, the most useful configuration is probably the combination of an ASCII controller and a network controller (Token Ring or Ethernet).

Most importantly, you have learned to manage and configure some of the key system resources. You should be able to alter report formatting to work better with your printer (CHGPRTF) and manage system notifications in a convenient manner (WRKRPYLE) that will not be disruptive to the System Operator. You should be comfortable working with the message queues (DSPMSG and WRKMSGQ) and the printer queues (WRKSPLF and WRKOUTQ). You have learned some important function keys to help you use AS/400 commands:

F1 help
F4 prompt
F5 refresh
F6 add
F9 all parameters
F11 keywords

The commands are:

CHGPRTF	change printer file (report attributes)
DSPMSG	display messages
WRKMSGQ	work with message queue
WRKOUTQ	work with output queue
WRKRPYLE	work with reply list entries
WRKSPLF	work with spooled files (printer queue)

3

AS/400 Connectivity

Once you are comfortable working with the AS/400's basic housekeeping features, it is time to start configuring the connected devices. The initial workstation(s) connected to the AS/400 will be configured automatically, but you will need to help the AS/400 establish communications with the PCs. As with the previous section, you will need sufficient authorization (such as Security Officer) to change many of the parameters outlined in this section.

PC Support uses APPC/APPN (advanced program-to-program communications and advanced peer-to-peer networking) to establish communications between the PC and the AS/400. APPC and APPN are very similar to each other; both are based on the Systems Network Architecture (SNA) logical unit 6.2 and node type 2.1 (usually referred to as SNA LU 6.2 or just LU 6.2). LU 6.2 is simply a connectivity standard that allows two systems to communicate in a distributed processing environment. APPC is the name of the feature that implements LU 6.2 on a system. Thus, a program that uses LU 6.2 to communicate with another system is said to have APPC Support. APPN adds features to APPC that make the network easier to configure and manage. As you configure PC Support, you may see APPC, APPN, and/or LU appear as references or portions of names.

INITIAL CONFIGURATION

When you install PC Support on your system, you will be asked for a few of the APPC/APPN details that affect your PC-to-AS/400 connection. The primary task you will face will be establishing naming conventions for your network so that the computers can "find" each other. There are, however, a few hardware details you may need to know for the initial configuration.

Logical Network Addresses

Each system on your network will need a name, known as the local LU name (or local logical unit name). Some people, especially on smaller networks, like to use names with personality such as planets (Mars, Saturn, Jupiter, etc.), colors (Gold, Silver, Blue, Green), or some other such scheme. In larger installations, it is often more convenient to use a descriptive name. For example, the MIS department might have a computer room with several PCs. A name such as M1120P02 could identify MIS Room 1120 PC number 2. Names are limited to eight characters, so if you select such a notation, you may need some terse and somewhat cryptic abbreviations.

If you are installing a new system, you may want to develop a naming plan ahead of time. As an example, consider a few of the names used at DK Micro and Rochester Systems Advisors:

RSA01—The AS/400 at RSA
PS2#55#1—The RSA PS/2 Model 55
AS400DK1—The AS/400 at DK Micro
PS2M80—DK Micro PS/2 Model 80
N486SP33—The 33-MHz 486 PC at DK Micro

In addition to the system names, there is also a network name. The network name default is APPN. Unless you will be connecting to a wide area network (WAN) consisting of several smaller APPC/APPN networks, you should leave the network name set to APPN. The complete address (as seen by APPN applications) is the combination of the network name and the location name with a period between the two parts. Thus, the Model 80 at DK Micro has a complete logical network address (name) of APPN.PS2M80.

PC Support must be told how to associate these logical names with the physical connection between the systems. When you install PC Support, you will specify the adapter type, such as Token Ring, Ethernet, Asynchronous (RS-232), Twinax, SDLC, or X.25, and the adapter address. For the direct connections, such as Twinax and SDLC, the address is simply the port number. For the local area network adapters (Token Ring and Ethernet), the address is the adapter's unique ID. Since you are probably working with (or planning to build) a PC local area network (LAN), a few more details about this address are worth knowing.

Every Token Ring or Ethernet adapter is built with a unique address (the manufacturer receives these addresses from a central "bank" to prevent duplicates across different product lines). This scheme can simplify installation—you would not need to generate physical addresses, as opposed to the logical addresses already discussed, for every system on your network. In addition, some software can automatically detect and use these addresses to simplify further the LAN installation process. When you install your network software (e.g., PC Support, OS/2 LAN Server, Extended Services) you will have a choice between using the built-in (universal) adapter address or specifying your own.

Physical Network Addresses

There are a few reasons why you might want to specify your own addresses. By using your own numbering system, you can generate a more meaningful name (e.g., by following room/location numbers or serial numbers). Many of the configuration utilities require that you provide the adapter address, and it may be simpler to recall your own address than look up the manufacturer's. There is also a maintenance aspect. If an adapter fails and you are using the universal address, you will need to reconfigure any software that does not automatically read the adapter address. Similarly, if a system is moved to another location, system-wide network maps may need updating. Using programmable addresses can greatly simplify network maintenance and troubleshooting.

As a practical example, consider Brad's office at DK Micro. There are three PCs in the office: An old PC using DOS, a PS/2 Model 80 using OS/2 2.0, and a 386 network server using OS/2 2.0 LAN Server. These computers are connected to the other PCs and the AS/400 through a Token Ring network. Token Ring user-defined addresses are selectable from the 400000000000–40007FFFFFFF range. Because this network was originally based on the LAN Server, the server was given the first address: 400000000000. As a concession to Brad, he was given the first 1000 addresses. Some of the address assignments in the office are:

400000000000	386 Server
400000000001	PS/2 Model 80 (primary workstation)
400000000002	PC (terminal and word processing)
400000001000	486 PC in the next office

All addresses up to 40006FFFFFFF were reserved for PCs. The 40007xxxxxxx addresses were reserved for minicomputers. Address 4001 was coded into this location to mean AS/400 number 1.

The AS/400's logging facilities keep track of the network adapters that connect and disconnect from the network. With a numbering system like this, it is easy to track network activity and, in the case of a problem, locate the offending machine.

This numbering system simplifies network upgrades. At one point, the 386 Server was upgraded to a 486. Simultaneously, the Token Ring adapter was upgraded from a standard model to a bus-master model. The new server was assigned 400000000000. The old server was moved to a new location (and new function) and assigned a new address. Thus, 40000000000 continued to designate the primary server.

CONFIGURING THE AS/400

After you have designed an addressing and naming scheme for the network, you can turn your attention to configuring the systems. First, you must prepare the AS/400 to accept PC connections. As with other hardware connections, the AS/400 can automatically configure the PC connection once you have established the basic parameters.

The Network ID

The default AS/400 configuration uses the serial number as the network name. You can view the current settings with the DSPNETA command [or DSPNETA OUTPUT(*PRINT) to send the configuration to the printer]. If you decide to change this name, use CHGNETA with the prompt key (F4), and change the system name to the new value; you may also change network name (Local Network ID) from APPN if you wish. Note: The new names will not take effect until the system is rebooted (IPLed).

If you are using a network adapter, you may have noticed that the adapter address does not appear in the network attributes. The network attributes apply to the logical (APPC/APPN) values, not the physical description of the network devices.

Line Descriptions

The details about AS/400 communications connections are called *line descriptions*. Network communications devices such as Token Ring and Ethernet have associated line descriptions. You can display (and change) these descriptions with the WRKLIND command. Using the change option (2) you can modify the adapter address, speed (for devices that support multiple data rates), and other hardware attributes. For now, the adapter address and link speed are the critical parameters. If your AS/400 has already been configured, you can use the display option (5) to see the current settings; you will need the adapter address when you configure PC Support. If the line description you need for PC Support attachment does not exist, you should log in as the Security Officer and select option 11 from the menu (PC Support Tasks). Now select option 22 (Configure PC Connections) and choose the appropriate adapter type. The AS/400 will prompt for a line name and query whether to add a PC to the line. The system will finish by prompting for specific device parameters such as the adapter address, data rate, and/or port address.

If you have autoconfiguration enabled, many of the parameters will be automatically selected. The AS/400 default setting has autoconfiguration enabled; you should probably leave it enabled (and answer "Y" to the "Auto create controller" prompt) unless you have a very good idea of what you are doing. If autoconfiguration is off, you will need to supply specific information about the PC you are connecting (PC adapter address, controller description, etc.).

The menus take care of many of the nitty-gritty details that you normally need not consider. However, if you need to display or change the line descriptions created during this process, you can use the WRKLIND command (work with line descriptions). This may be particularly important if you must change a parameter that PC Support configuration does not prompt for (e.g., the Token Ring data rate if you need a 4-MHz rate, rather than a 16-MHz rate).

Authorizing Users

This takes care of the physical connection information, but you still must deal with the system security. If a PC can use the AS/400 as a file server, then it naturally has potential access to a wealth of data. Without security provisions on PC access, user security could be bypassed. So, the AS/400 requires that the PC Support user log into the system just as any other user would. You can add a PC Support user with option 21 (Enroll PC Support Users).

The system will prompt you for a user profile, user ID, address, and description. The user profile is the name the user enters to log in. The user ID is the name the network will use to identify the user. Most people will use the same name for both the profile and the ID. The address is simply the name of the computer set in the net attributes. Following the examples above, to enroll a user named BRADLEY the values would be:

User profile:	BRADLEY
User identifier	
User ID:	BRADLEY
Address:	AS400DK

The user description will appear next to the ID when you view or change user lists. There are two strategies you can follow when assigning users to PC Support. First, you can use the same profile for both interactive terminal use and PC Support tasks. This strategy is useful when there is a tight integration between tasks on the PC and AS/400, and this is probably the goal you will be pursuing.

You should probably create separate user profiles for PC Support and general log-in tasks (although the same profile may be used for both tasks). By using separate profiles, you can place tighter restrictions on the PC Support ID. Since the PC Support sessions will often tend to stay connected for longer periods, the risk of damage from unauthorized use (e.g., someone using another person's system while they are away from the desk) are lessened. Furthermore, separate IDs will create separate message queues for the two functions. You may find it more convenient to handle messages through the workstation interface than the PC Support menu; with a separate log-in name for the workstation, you can have your messages appear there.

You can display the user list with the WRKUSRPRF command (work with user profiles). To add a user, type 1 in the option column and the new name in the user column. You will see several options. For now, there are only two parameters that are particularly important. First, you can restrict a user to menu navigation only (no command line entries) by entering "Y" for "Restrict command line use." Second, you can set the access authority at the "Type of user" prompt. The possible selections, from most restrictions to least, are:

*USER
*PGMR
*SYSOPR
*SECADM
*SECOFR

You may also want to enter a description that gives basic information about the user (such as the full name). The default password will be the user ID unless otherwise specified. If you accept the default, the user will be prompted for a new password after the first log in. If you need more control over profile creation, particularly when tailoring higher security access, you can use the CRTUSRPRF command. In addition to the type of user (user class), you may specify Special Authorities which grant a user additional system privileges.

As your system grows, there are more convenient ways to create new user profiles. Rather than building a profile from scratch, you can create unused template profiles for the various user categories. Then, you simply use option 3 to copy the template to the new user name.

Configuring the PCs

You can configure PC Support for DOS or OS/2. Most of the examples and discussion in this book will center on the OS/2 version of PC Support, because it has several advantages over the DOS version. Most importantly, OS/2 2.0 gives your DOS programs more access to memory. Where the DOS version may leave only 400–500 K of the critical base memory free, an OS/2 virtual DOS session can leave 630 K or more base memory while running PC Support, LAN software, and even other DOS programs in multiple windows.

There are some restrictions you should take into consideration before selecting OS/2 2.0 as your PC Support platform, however. You will need Extended Services for OS/2 (a separate product) in order to use PC Support. On the hardware side, OS/2 2.0 requires at least an 80386 processor, and you should have at least 8 Mb of RAM, and 30–40 Mb of free disk space. Technically, less memory (and hard disk space) is required, but the performance with less than 8 Mb is not sufficiently fast for most people.

If your machine does not meet these requirements, you should request an upgrade. If an upgrade is not possible, you should install the DOS version. With the DOS version, you can configure an extended memory version if your system has more than 1 Mb of RAM (the preferred configuration) or the standard version if you have less than 1 Mb. In either case, be prepared to boot your system without PC Support for programs that will not have enough free memory available when PC Support is running.

Whichever platform you choose, there are a few key attributes you should know before installing PC Support: The network adapter type, the physical address and logical address (name) of the AS/400, and the logical address (name) of your PC. If you are using a network adapter, you may also need the physical address of the adapter (unless you are using the burned-in address, which is not recommended). Synchronous and asynchronous connections require further details about line rates and switching.

If you are coming to the AS/400 from a PC background, you are probably working with, or should be considering, a network configuration. So, the examples will follow a Token Ring network installation. Ethernet installation is nearly identical, although there will be additional physical address constraints if you use LAN bridges (this information can be found in the *PC Support Installation and Administration Guide*).

PC Support for DOS

IBM distributes two sets of diskettes for the DOS version of PC Support. One set is the standard DOS version, the other is the extended DOS version. If you have a 286 or higher PC with extended memory available, you should choose the extended DOS version; it is faster and leaves more base memory free for your DOS applications. The labels on the two sets of diskettes are not very clear. Near the center of the label, one of the lines will read either "IBM PC Support/400 V2 DOS" or "IBM PC Support/400 V2 DOS Extended." Make sure all of the diskettes in the set you are using have the same label (it is possible to install a mixed set, but the program will not run properly after installation).

Network Adapter Configuration

If you will be using Token Ring or Ethernet, you must install the network drivers before installing PC Support. IBM distributes these drivers as a product, called the LAN Support Program. If you are using an adapter from another vendor, you may need to substitute one or more drivers for DXMC0MOD.SYS. The LAN Support program includes an install utility, DXMAID, which copies the appropriate .SYS files and adds the following lines to CONFIG.SYS (where *D:* is the letter and path where the .SYS files are located and *address* is the physical address to be assigned to the adapter):

```
DEVICE=D:\DXMA0MOD.SYS
DEVICE=D:\DXMC0MOD.SYS address
```

As a specific example, the DK Micro Model 80 referenced earlier would use:

```
DEVICE=C:\DXMA0MOD.SYS
DEVICE=C:\DXMC0MOD.SYS 400000000001
```

Ethernet uses DXME0MOD.SYS in place of DXMC0MOD.SYS, but is otherwise identical.

If your computer is already configured with network drivers, or you use the DXMAID program to install the system, you may see a line with the DXMT0MOD.SYS driver. This is the NETBIOS driver, which is not required for PC Support. If PC Support is the only program using the network adapter (e.g., you are not also using a LAN program), you can remove the DXMT0MOD line to save a little memory.

If the drivers were not previously installed, you should reboot the system after driver installation. This will load the network device drivers and allow you to test the PC Support connection when you complete the next stage of installation.

Drive Selections

After entering A:INSTALL, the program will prompt for the name of your PC Support drive (location of the PC Support directory) and boot drive. The boot drive location is used for modifying the CONFIG.SYS and AUTOEXEC.BAT files. The actual PC Support program and data files will be transferred to the PC Support drive—the install program will name the directory \PCS.

PC Support Startup Options

Next, you will be asked whether PC Support should start automatically; i.e., whether it will be added to the AUTOEXEC.BAT file and load each time the system is booted. If most of your work will require AS/400 access, you should probably select automatic start. On the other hand, if you have many critical programs that require large amounts of base memory, you may want to disable automatic startup and teach your users to start PC Support when needed.

The next prompt, "Reduce messages displayed when starting PC Support," adds an "ECHO OFF" line to the batch file if you answer Yes. If you like to see what is happening within the batch file, you should select No.

You can select which module PC Support initially displays after loading the PC Support menu, the Organizer menu, the OfficeVision/400 menu, the AS/400 initial menu, or the DOS command prompt. The first two are shells that present PC Support DOS (PC Support menu) or AS/400 (Organizer menu) tasks in a menu format. These may be useful to novice users who have a few, selected tasks to accomplish. The OfficeVision/400 menu is a more restrictive version of the AS/400 Organizer menu. It presents an AS/400 log-in screen and proceeds directly to OfficeVision (if installed on the AS/400) after the user logs in.

The AS/400 initial screen loads the workstation feature (terminal emulation) and proceeds to the AS/400 menu after the user logs in. This option is handy for the advanced user who works primarily on the AS/400 and occasionally with DOS. If you come from a PC background, you should probably select the DOS command prompt option. This will load PC support and return to the DOS prompt.

Supplementary Functions

Next, you should select any additional PC Support functions that should be loaded during startup. The virtual printer option lets the PC use a printer attached to the AS/400 as if it were connected to the PC. Because the AS/400 tends to have limited printing capabilities (compared to a PC), you probably will not use this option. More likely, you will make your PC printer accessible to the AS/400; this is a function of the Workstation Function.

The Message Function sends and receives messages to and from other AS/400 users. If you will not be using the Workstation Function (described next), you can use the Message Function to manage the messages. However, if you are using the Workstation Function it is preferable to use messaging from a terminal session, as the Message Function would further reduce the available base memory on the PC.

The Workstation Function provides terminal emulation (and printer) capabilities. You can configure up to five concurrent sessions, individually selectable as terminals and/or printers. Most users will find a single terminal and printer session sufficient. However, programmers and system administrators may prefer two or more terminal sessions. Multiple sessions can greatly enhance problem determination and debugging tasks.

The Workstation Function will run as a TSR (terminate and stay resident) application on the PC. You can move back and forth between the terminal emulation and DOS prompt (or current DOS program) with the Alt-Esc key.

Connection Configuration

After configuring the PC Support options, the install program will prompt for the connection parameters. This is where you will need several of the addresses and hardware attributes outlined earlier.

If you are using a Token Ring (or Ethernet) connection, select "Local-Area Network" as the connection type. You will be prompted for the PC location name, system information (AS/400 name), and system LAN address (physical address of the LAN adapter on the AS/400). For the DK Micro Model 80 used in previous examples, these parameters would be:

PC Location Name:	APPN.PS2M80
System Information:	AS400DK1
System LAN Address:	400070004001

When you have finished entering the information, you will be asked whether or not to attempt a connection to the AS/400. This gives you a chance to test the connection. (If you are using a network connection, the drivers must already be loaded.) If the test does not work, you may need to change the configuration. If it does work, you must reboot the PC before you can actually use PC Support.

PC Support Configuration Files

If the test connection did not work, or you want to change connection parameters, it is sometimes simpler to edit the configuration files rather than use the PC Support menus. Most of the critical parameters are stored in the \PCS\CONFIG.PCS file, although a few parameters may be found in the PCs CONFIG.SYS, such as the adapter drivers and addressing, as mentioned earlier.

PC Support for OS/2

If you have an OS/2-capable system, PC Support for OS/2 is a far better choice than the DOS version, even if all of the applications you run on the PC use DOS. OS/2 gives your DOS applications the resources they need to run efficiently and effectively. Installing PC Support for OS/2 is a bit more complicated than DOS, but well worth the effort. The added complexity comes from PC Support's reliance on Extended Services (aka Communications Manager) for establishing and managing the connection between the PC and the AS/400. Where PC Support for DOS provides the drivers and workstation feature, under OS/2, Extended Services is responsible for the drivers and terminal emulation. Thus, PC Support for OS/2 has fewer modules than its DOS counterpart. OS/2 Extended Services is a far more advanced product than the rudimentary functions provide by DOS PC Support. Using Extended Services, you can configure the OS/2-based PC as a full-fledged APPN node of any type. These advanced features can make installation much more complex. When you install Extended Services, you will have a choice between "advanced" and "basic" installation. While it may be tempting to select advanced, particularly if you are a very experienced PC user, the installation will run much more quickly and with fewer problems if you select basic. Fortunately, reconfiguring a basic installation to take advantage of advanced features is a relatively simple task; indeed, you will probably find it much simpler to alter a working, basic configuration than start off with an advanced configuration.

Extended Services Installation

The installation process starts with the ESINST.CMD file (type "A:ESINST" from the OS/2 command line, or double click the mouse on the ESINST icon in drive A:). After copying a few diskettes and displaying some informational screens, the installation program prompts you for either basic, advanced, or custom installation. Custom installation is designed for administrators who design a specific configuration diskette for the end user. The end user selects custom and leaves the real work to the installation program (and the administrator who built the diskette). So, unless you are using the AS/400 as part of a large department, you will probably need basic or advanced.

Keep in mind that a basic installation may later be modified to include all of the features of an advanced installation. By far your safest strategy is to use basic installation to get a working connection to the AS/400 and make advanced modifications (if needed) at a later time.

Although basic installation may sound like a simple process, there are quite a few details you must know ahead of time. This includes such items as the type of communications adapter (including the model), adapter address, and the printer model. After selecting basic you will be prompted for a configuration file name. This configuration file will be unique to each PC connected to the AS/400. Hence, it is generally a good idea to give the configuration file a name related to the workstation. For example, the first computer for Department 12 in Room 340 could be named D12R340A. After entering a name, you will be prompted for a comment line. You can simply leave the comment as BASIC CONFIGURATION FILE, for now.

The install will then lead you through a series of configuration options. Your first choice concerns the type(s) of terminal emulation you need to configure. The 5250 Workstation Function (selected with the "W" key) is the proper emulation mode for connecting to an AS/400. Although you can revisit this installation screen to add the other options, such as 3270 and ASCII emulation, you should probably keep things simple and select only the 5250 configuration. As with advanced options, you can always modify the installation later to configure additional features.

The configuration screen is shown in Figure 3.1. You can access up to four 5250 terminal sessions plus a printer session simultaneously. A typical user would require only one session. But if you are a programmer or system administrator, you may want several sessions, one for writing programs, one for running programs, one for administration, and so forth. Or, if you have several AS/400s at your site, you could configure a session for each host computer.

The printer session allows the AS/400 to access a printer attached to the local computer. If you will be using a printer connected directly to the AS/400 or a printer attached to another computer, you should answer no for the 5250 printer session.

You should also select the connection type (for the purposes of this example, a Token Ring LAN was selected) and the host computer (AS/400).

```
                  5250 Workstation Function Defaults


Use the spacebar to change 5250 Workstation Function selections.
An arrow is displayed next to the option when it is selected.
Press Enter when you have completed the sections.

Number of 5250 host sessions. . . . . . . . . . . . . <141> 1      <144> 2
                                                      <144> 3      <144> 4
5250 printer session. . . . . . . . . . . . . . . . . <141> Yes
                                                      <144> No
Connection type . . . . . . . . . . . . . . . . . . . <144> Twinax
                                                      <141> LAN
                                                      <144> SDLC
Host type . . . . . . . . . . . . . . . . . . . . . . <141> AS/400
                                                      <144> S/36


Enter  Esc=Cancel  F1=Help
```

Figure 3.1 Configuration screen

Workstation Function Sessions (Terminal and Printer)

After answering this basic configuration information, the installation program will continue prompting for details. If you have configured a printer, the program will prompt you for a printer type (5256, 5224, or 5219). The 5219 is the most generic type available. After selecting the type you must specify the connection (LPT1, LPT2, etc.) and the printer model (Proprinter and Wheelprinter are generally acceptable for dot matrix and laser printers, respectively). Next you will be prompted for details about the PC-to-host connection. For LAN connections you must enter the type of network: Token Ring, Ethernet (which IBM calls ETHERAND), IBM PC Network, or 3174 Peer Communications Network. You may also be prompted for the adapter type (e.g., Token Ring, Token Ring II, or Token Ring 16/4). You should also decide whether to use the universal address or specify a locally administered (custom) address for the adapter. As mentioned earlier, there are several advantages to a locally administered address; if you select this option, you must take care not to assign the same address to more than one system.

Perhaps the most disconcerting screen for new Communications Manager users follows the adapter details. The installation program prompts for four details: The local LU name, the partner LU name, the mode name, and the LAN destination address. To most users, the LAN destination address is the most obvious. It is the LAN adapter address of the AS/400; in the case of the example for DK Micro cited earlier, this would be 400070004001.

The two LU names are the network names you assigned earlier when developing a naming scheme. The local name is the name of your system and the partner name is the name of the AS/400. It is helpful to use the same name for the local LU that you used for the configuration file name; D12R340A for this example. And, referring back to the example for DK Micro, the partner name was AS400DK1. The mode name is established by PC Support and should be set to QPCSUPP.

The next screen prompts for several additional details and you should simply accept the defaults assigned by the installation program. The local node name will default to the local LU name you specified on the previous screen, the network ID will default to APPN (this should only be changed if your system is part of a larger wide-area network), and the local node ID should default to the proper value.

When you return to the initial installation screen, simply hit F3 to continue the process, unless you really want to go to the trouble of installing additional services at this point. After prompting for the destination drive for the Communications Manager files, the installation program takes over, prompting for additional diskettes and configuring additional network details automatically. The full APPN naming conventions can become quite complex. Fortunately, basic installation handles the really messy stuff for you. Indeed, if you later delve into advanced installation (options available through the main Configuration Manager screen) you will see a number of additional parameters such as local LU alias, partner LU alias, and a host of additional network IDs and names. The first time you start Communications Manager, it will prompt you for the name of the configuration file; D12R340A for the purposes of this example. Should you ever need to change anything, the alias function is quite useful, if a bit confusing at first.

PC Support installs a core set of programs and data files on your local hard disk. If you are using an adapter with a slow data rate or a network with a large traffic load, you may want to install additional functions on the local disk.

SUMMARY

In this chapter you learned the rudiments of connectivity with the AS/400, such as using APPC/APPN and LU 6.2; configuring PC Support; using logical and physical network addresses; working with line descriptions; and configuring network connections and adaptors. You saw the differences between PC Support for DOS and PC Support for OS/2, and how to configure and install each.

You have also learned the following commands:

CHGNETA	change network attributes
CRTUSRPRF	create user profile
DSPNETA	display network attributes
WRKLIND	work with line descriptions
WRKUSRPRF	work with user profiles

4

Introduction to the System Architecture

Now that you can handle some basic system management tasks on the AS/400, it is time to take a closer look at the development and application environment. Here the departure from a PC environment, or for that matter, most other computer systems, is quite radical. On the PC, you may be quite familiar with the hierarchical storage system: The directory tree. In contrast, the AS/400 follows a concept called single level store. There are no directory trees to navigate. There is one caveat, however. PC Support and some applications (e.g., the OfficeVision products) use a hierarchical storage system to help maintain compatibility across different system architectures.

LIBRARIES

You may already be thinking, "No directories? Maintaining this system is going to be a nightmare with all of those files stored at a single level!" But it is not that bad. There are many *libraries* used to organize your files. In some respects, a library is similar to a DOS directory—it holds files. But unlike a directory, a library cannot contain another library. In earlier chapters, you have already seen a few libraries, such as the QSYS library, where the report definitions for command output are stored. When you wanted to change the attributes of an entire set of reports, you typed CHGPRTF QSYS/*ALL (change the attributes of all print files in the QSYS library)—not all that different from a DOS or OS/2 command such as ATTRIB \DIR1*.* -H (remove hidden attributes from all files in the \DIR1 directory).

You should keep several different objectives in mind when creating libraries. Objectives might include security, program development, file maintenance, departmentalization, and backup/recovery procedures. Security is a concern for sensitive data such as a company's financial data. The financial data files could be kept in a library with restricted access. Developers will probably keep programming projects in separate libraries to keep programs organized. Yet, in a database system, many programs may need access to a common set of files. Therefore, database files (physical and logical files) may be kept in one or more libraries.

Likewise, multiple departments may use the same program to work with different data sets; the departments may share a common program library and use different data libraries. Finally, it may be simpler to reconstruct some large files rather than waste time (and space) running a backup. Such files could be kept in a library that is not subject to daily backups.

The Library List

As you can see from these examples, your programs and data may not be located in the same library. Just as DOS provides a path to access programs stored in multiple directories, the AS/400 has a *library list* that lets the user run programs in multiple libraries. However, the library list is more all-encompassing than the DOS path; it also affects data files (similar to the DOS APPEND). Thus, if the file you want is stored in a library that appears in your library list, you need only name the file to work with it. This is extremely useful when working with large databases.

The library list is also handy for application development. You can keep test data in one library and actual working data in another. During program development, the library list would include the test library. Then, when the program is finished, the list entry for the test data would be changed to the library name of the actual data, assuming the programmer needs access to actual data. All through the development cylce, the end users would have the actual data location in their library lists and would never need be affected by the development cycle.

You can see the current library list by entering the DSPLIBL command. The display might look something like this:

```
Opt   Library    Type   Text
_     QSYS       SYS    System Library
_     QSYS2      SYS    System Library for CPIs
_     QHLPSYS    SYS    Help Library
_     QUSRSYS    SYS    System Library for Users
_     MYLIB      CUR    Current Development Library
_     QGPL       USR    General Purpose Library
_     QTEMP      USR    User Library
```

Note that several library types appear in the list, such as system, current, and user. Most libraries are either system or user libraries—commands and data needed for system data or user-specific entries, respectively. The current library is limited to a single entry and is intended as a temporary entry; it has priority over the user libraries so that new programs or files (or those under development for programmers) have precedence over older, tested versions. If you run into a serious bug and need the older version, you can simply remove the current library entry.

A fourth library type, called the product library (PRD), has precedence over all but the system library. The product library may be used by commercial applications you install on the system. By keeping the priority of system and product libraries higher than user-defined data and programs, the system avoids redefinition problems. Consider a user who writes a program and gives it the name of a system command. Because system commands have a higher priority, AS/400 will continue to behave as normal, and the new user program will not run. Contrast this to DOS or OS/2, where a similar mistake might temporarily disable a system command.

You can modify the user portion of the library list with the EDTLIBL command. Each library in the list has a sequence number—the lower the number, the higher the priority. Thus, if files or programs in different libraries share the same name, the object in the lower numbered library is used. You can override the numbers in the display screen by typing over them (e.g., enter sequence 001, 002, 003, etc.).

BUILDING A DATABASE

Now it is time to get down to some real work! You have access to a machine designed for database work; it is time to define a simple database file. First, you will create a library for your work. In the following example the library name will be MYDBLIB (for "my database library"). Enter CRTLIB followed by F4 and fill in the screen as follows:

```
Create Library (CRTLIB)
Library:            MYDBLIB
Library type:       *TEST
Text "description": My test database
```

You could add the library to the user list with the EDTLIB command. But with only one library name to add it is quicker to use another command: ADDLIBLE MYDBLIB. By default, the add library list entry command places the named library at the head of the user list. You may, however, specify the position as *LAST or relative to a library already in the list:

```
ADDLIBLE MYDBLIB *LAST
ADDLIBLE MYDBLIB POSITION(*AFTER QGPL)
ADDLIBLE MYDBLIB POSITION(*BEFORE QGPL)
```

Now you can create a database file. On the AS/400, a database file is a compiled object. First, you must write the source code that describes the file. This is called the DDS (Data Description Specification). The DDS is then compiled to create the actual database file. As with source code on a PC, the DDS is not used by the resulting file.

The changes you make to the library list with EDTLIBL and ADDLIBLE are not permanent; they last only for the current session. If you will be working extensively with a library (e.g., for database development), you should make the library a permanent part of your environment. To make the changes permanent, you must modify the job description that loads when you log on (or more likely, the security officer must change the job description).

A Quick Tour of the Programming Development Manager

If you are an experienced programmer on the PC, you are probably using a development system to edit, compile, and debug programs. Examples of such environments include Microsoft's Software Development Kit and IBM's Workset/2. On the AS/400, the tool of choice is the PDM (Programming Development Manager), which is part of the Application Development Tools software package. To start PDM, enter:

```
STRPDM
```

You are now at the main PDM menu. Since MYDBLIB is a new library, you will need to create a file for your source code by using the create source physical file command (CRTSRCPF). The primary database files on the AS/400 are called *physical files*. Until you become thoroughly familiar with the AS/400, you should always use QDDSSRC as the file name for your physical file source code.

```
CRTSRCPF MYDBLIB/QDDSSRC
```

Once you have created the DDS source file, you can add a DDS description to the file. Select option 3 (Work with Members). You will be prompted for a file name, library name, member name, and type. For now, you should always use QDDSSRC as the name of a DDS source file. You will be working with several file members (*ALL) of all types (also *ALL). So the entry screen would be filled in as follows:

```
File:         QDDSSRC
Library:      MYDBLIB
Member Name:  *ALL
Member Type:  *ALL
```

The next screen displays the *members* of the QDDSSRC file. Since MYDBLIB is a newly created file, it has no members, and the display reports "No members in file." Unlike DOS, where each source code module is stored in a separate file, AS/400 can store several source code modules (DDSs) in a single file. That is one reason for using a generic name, such as QDDSSRC, for your source code files. The actual source code names are differentiated by member names.

Now you can create a DDS by hitting the F6 (create) key. In this example, the database will store address information, so ADDRESS would be an appropriate source member name. It will be source code for a physical file, and thus the source type will be PF. Thus, you would use the following entries:

```
Source file:         QDDSSRC
Library:             MYDBLIB
Source member:       ADDRESS
Source type:         PF
Text "description":  ADDRESS database
```

A Quick Tour of the Source Entry Utility

This starts another program called the SEU (Source Entry Utility). The SEU is an editor. Unlike typical PC-based editors, the SEU supports strict formatting conventions and syntax checking. The screen contains a boxed-in area with room for line numbers along the left side of the screen. Across the top of the data area, you will see labels A, T, Name, R, Len, T, Dp, B, and F. The field definitions must be aligned with these column headings (the SEU adjusts the headings and syntax checking to the source file type entered in the previous step). To enter a new line of source code, move the cursor to the dots in the left column and type IP (for insert in prompted mode). You can now enter a line of source code.

Rather than formatting the information manually, prompted mode gives you a miniature entry form for your data. Now you will see descriptions for each of the column labels listed above the data area: Name type, name, ref, length, data type, decimal positions, use, and functions. Before you begin entering the description, you should have a general design for your database file. If you are following standard relational database design conventions, every database file (table) should have a unique key. For an address database, this unique key might be a client number. Of course, a client may have more than one office, so you might prefer a two-field key: client number and sub entry number (CLINUM and SUBENT, respectively). You will also need fields for the general information: Courtesy title, first name, last name, company name, address line 1, address line 2, city, state, and zip code. Depending on your application, you may also want some general information such as a telephone number.

Building the DDS

If you will be using a unique key, as in this example, the first line in the DDS must specify the "unique" function. So, use the field exit key (the right ctrl key on most PC keyboards) to move to the "functions" heading and enter "unique." When you hit the Enter key, the editor automatically moves to the next line of source code. Every record definition on the AS/400 should have a name; you can call the address record ADDREC. The address record requires a special name type (R), so type "R" under name type and ADDREC under name. You are now ready to begin entering the field definitions.

Field definitions do not require a name type. However, you must enter a field name, length, and data type. Most of the ADDRESS fields will be alphanumeric (data type A). The length specifies the number of characters in the field. You may want a numeric field for SUBENT. The most common numeric type on the AS/400 is packed decimal (coded as "P"). The length of a packed decimal number specifies the number of digits, and the decimal position specifies the number of digits after the decimal point. You can use the names and attributes in Table 4.1 for the ADDRESS field defintions.

You should list the key fields at the end of the DDS. Key fields use a name type of "K" followed by the name of the field. If you are using multiple field keys, the fields should be listed in the order of precedence (e.g., CLINUM followed by SUBENT).

Remember to use the field exit key (Ctrl) rather than the tab key to move from one field to the next. The field completion key aligns the entry properly before moving to the next field. If you use the tab key, the field entries may not be aligned properly and the SEU will complain (the length and decimal position fields must be right aligned).

TABLE 4.1 ADDRESS Field Definitions

Name	*Type*	*Length*	*Decimal Positions*
CLINUM	A	10	
SUBENT	P	2	0
CT	A	4	
FIRST	A	12	
LAST	A	20	
COMPANY	A	30	
ADD1	A	30	
ADD2	A	30	
CITY	A	20	
STATE	A	3	
ZIP	A	7	
TELEPHONE	A	14	

When you have finished entering the definition, you should hit F3 to exit. You will be asked to confirm the change/create of the file member; accept the default, Y. The "Work with Members" screen appears and includes the new DDS, ADDRESS. You now have a source file for the physical file, but the physical file has not yet been created. To create the file, you must compile the source; with PDM, simply type 14 (Compile) in the option column of the member you wish to compile (ADDRESS). The system will print a report listing the source code and errors (if any). If there were errors, you can simply enter 2 (Edit) next to the DDS name and the system returns to the SEU.

The preceding process may seem a bit awkward. It may help if you keep the following model in mind when working with AS/400 database files. Building a database file on the AS/400 is similar to the source code edit/compile cycle on a PC. The SEU acts as the source code editor and the PDM gives you convenient access to the compiler (option 14). Just as you must save source code if you want to later change a program, so you must save DDS source. Similarly, if you change DDS source, you must recompile before the changes take effect.

THE DATA FILE UTILITY

There are many ways to enter data into your newly created ADDRESS file. For now, you can use the Data File Utility (DFU), another module in the Application Development Tools. Fortunately, the command line is available from most PDM screens, so you can easily access the DFU with the STRDFU command. From the DFU menu, select option 2—Create a DFU program. You must then enter the program name, program library, data file name (e.g., the file for which you are designing the screen), and the data file library. For example, you might name the ADDRESS data entry program ADDENTRY. Following the examples cited earlier, the prompts would be filled in as:

```
Program:    ADDENTRY
Library:    MYDBLIB

Data file: ADDRESS
Library:    MYDBLIB
```

Next, the system will prompt for a job title ("Address Entry Program" will work nicely) and several options. For now, most of the options can be left at their default values. However, if "Audit Report" is defaulting to "Y," you might want to change it to "N." The audit report prints a report of all changes made to the data file when program execution ends. While this may be handy for some applications, it can be quite annoying when not required, as in this example.

The next screen lists the record formats for the ADDRESS file. In this example, the ADDRESS file has only one record format: ADDREC. Select the record definition by placing option 2 (Specify) next to ADDREC and hit Enter. The next screen displays the field names for the records. You can use this form to select records to include on the data entry screen. For now, hit the F21 key to select all fields; this will number the fields from 1 to 12. This *sequence number* determines the order that the fields will appear on the entry screen (you could, of course, manually enter numbers if you do not want the fields listed in the default order).

Now when you hit Enter, the system presents a list of headings (labels) for each field. You may also specify an extended definition (but you can ignore that option this time). If you are satisfied with the default headings, hit Enter. The next screen is similar to the SEU save screen. You can simply hit Enter again to accept the default (save the program). If you prefer, you could enter "Y" under "Save DDS Source" and type a name in the source file field before hitting Enter. This would save a copy of the source code for the data entry program. Then, if you wanted to add special features to the entry program (or use the Screen Design Aid to enhance the appearance) the source code would be available.

Data Entry

After saving the program, the system displays the "Change a Data File" screen. If you want to run the newly created entry program, simply hit Enter to accept the defaults. The system displays the entry fields, with key fields highlighted, and you can begin entering data. The mode, shown in the upper right corner of the screen, should be entry. If it is not, you can hit the F10 key to select entry mode. To enter records, simply key in the field values and hit Enter when the record is complete.

Data Modification

If you want to change an existing record, hit F11 to enter the change mode. The system will prompt for a key value; simply enter the key for the record you wish to change and the program will retrieve the current values. Depending on the field format, the program may be a bit finicky about the data alignment within the field. As with the prompted mode of SEU, it helps if you use the field exit key (right Ctrl) after entering each value. This will ensure that the field data is properly aligned.

If you do not know the key value, you can use PgUp and PgDn (called Roll Down and Roll Up by AS/400 users) to move through the existing records. Alternatively, you can enter your best guess. If the system displays an error (Record not found) you can then use PgUp and PgDn to move to the closest next or closest previous match.

When you have finished entering and changing records, simply hit F3 to exit the data entry program. The system will display the number of records added, changed, and deleted, and ask for confirmation that you wish to end the program. You will be returned to the main DFU menu, at which point you can run another program or hit F3 to exit.

DATABASE DESIGN

By now, you should have learned some of the basics behind working with database files on the AS/400. Certainly, there are many topics yet to cover, such as report design, query, and advanced screen design, to name a few. But before you start building larger files and applications, you should have a firm understanding of the database architecture and at least a general design from which to work.

The AS/400 architecture has many features in common with the relational model defined by E.F. Codd. While you may be familiar with so-called relational databases on the PC, you should be mindful of the fact that the term *relational* is used very loosely in the computer industry as a whole. A quick overview of relational concepts should help put things in perspective and provide a foundation for your database design goals. Although the AS/400 cannot be considered *fully relational*, many of its features are similar enough that relational design concepts can be applied.

Codd's earliest formal definition of the relational model included 12 rules for relational databases. Although the model was greatly expanded, as specified in his recent book, *The Relational Model for Database Management, Version 2* (Reading, MA: Addison-Wesley, 1990), the original 12 rules are a useful starting point. Indeed, until the newer ideas presented in Version 2 become widely implemented, the 12 rules will remain the primary standard for relational design.

Rule 0: The Fundamental Rule

This is not one of the original "12 rules," but rather a basic assumption about relational databases. Any database that claims to be relational must allow all database management tasks to be implemented through relational methods. The system can support nonrelational methods, but none of these nonrelational operations can be required to perform management tasks; i.e., they can only be optional management functions.

Rule 1: The Information Rule

- All data is accessed through values in base relations (physical files on the AS/400).
- The base relations may not have record numbers.
- Duplicate rows are not allowed (the unique keyword in the DDS would be a requirement rather than an option).
- The system may store information in any arbitrary order without affecting relational operations.
- The system supports derived relations (logical files on the AS/400). Derived relations are often called *views*.
- A derived relation behaves like a base relation except that the data may be stored in more than one base relation and the data may be ordered (sorted).

Rule 2: Guaranteed Access

Every value stored in a relation may be retrieved by specifying three parameters: The base relation name (physical file name), the column name (field name), and the primary key value (one or more field values that make up the unique key).

Rule 3: Missing Information

The database supports a *mark* that designates information in a field is unknown. The mark is not a value, but rather a flag that affects logical operations. Version 2 supports two different types of marks: Applicable, the information exists but is unknown, and inapplicable, the information does not exist. For example, your neighbor's dog's name is inapplicable if your neighbor does not own a dog and applicable if your neighbor has a dog, but you don't know its name.

Rule 4: Active Catalog

All information about the database is stored within the database. Thus information such as file names, column names, and view definitions are stored within relations. This allows the operator to query the database; e.g., does a specific type of data (field name) exist on the system?

Rule 5: Comprehensive Data Sublanguage

The database includes a query language that supports three- or four-value logic: True, false, and maybe; or true, false, maybe-applicable, and maybe-inapplicable. The query language must be capable of performing all types of database manipulation including data retrieval, updates, file definition, etc.

Rule 6: View Updateability

Reading a view (logical file) should be no different than reading a base relation (physical file). However, it is possible to define a view that cannot be written and maintain a consistent behavior when applying the changes or additions to the base relations. The system should make a reasonably thorough attempt to determine which views are updateable at definition time. Note that it is not possible to design a set of rules that will determine the updateability of all views.

Rule 7: High-Level Operations

Relational operations should be applicable to multiple records with only a single command; i.e., the query language cannot require programming loops to operate upon multiple records.

Rule 8: Physical Data Independence

Storage patterns and/or access paths (indexes) may be changed without affecting the logical operation of the database. Such changes should affect only the performance of the system.

Rule 9: Logical Data Independence

As long as physical changes to the base relations do not result in the loss of information, the logical structure of the relations may be changed without affecting existing programs or user interaction. Thus, base relations can be split or combined, and a view (derived relation) representing the old structure will be sufficient to maintain backward compatibility.

Rule 10: Integrity Independence

The database should allow rule definition (to specify acceptable data values) as part of the relation's properties. The rules can be changed without requiring the recompilation of existing programs (all programs will immediately implement the new rules). Furthermore, applications cannot bypass the rules.

Rule 11: Distribution Independence

Data can be redistributed to multiple machines without affecting application programs or user interaction.

Rule 12: Nonsubversion

A system may allow programs written in a language other than the DSL. However, if additional languages are supported, they may not bypass relational integrity and are subject to the same constraints as DSL applications.

BASIC ELEMENTS

The unique key value is an important feature of a relational database. By requiring a unique key, query results maintain a consistent behavior that is not possible with nonunique keys. Although the AS/400 does not use record number, it does allow duplicate key values in a physical file (base relation). IBM made an interesting compromise; the system maintains a unique identifier for each record that tracks the entry sequence. If the user does not request a unique key, the AS/400 uses this unique record identifier to maintain a key of sorts "under the covers." Technically, according to Codd, a unique sequence key should be user-specified action when no other unique attributes are applicable. You would be well advised to follow such a convention explicitly when designing files that have no other key.

The view or derived relation is another basic feature that appears in several of the rules. On the AS/400 this is called a logical file. At its simplest level, a logical file is simply another way of looking at a physical file—the only difference is the order in which the records are presented. In other words, the logical file uses a different sort order. On the AS/400, the term *key* is used unconventionally.

Usually, a key is presumed to be unique. On the AS/400, a key need not be unique and determines the indexed field(s). As an example, consider the ADDRESS file from the previous examples. There are several different ways a viewer might want this information presented. Someone working in billing might prefer the base definition with records presented in client number order. The person in the mailing room might prefer zip code order. And, if you are using the list as an address book, you probably prefer alphabetical order by company name. All of these preferences can be fulfilled through logical files.

Consider your preference for an alphabetical list. Not only do you have a list of clients, but some clients may have more than one person listed in the database. So, in addition to sorting the list by company name, you would like a secondary sort on last name (probably followed by first name). To create a logical file, first select "work with members" from the PDM. When you get to the SEU startup screen, you type the same information you entered for a physical file, except for one item. Now, instead of member type PF (physical file), you enter member type LF (logical file):

```
File:         QDDSSRC
  Library:  MYDBLIB

Member
  Name:       *ALL
  Type:       LF
```

For the source member name, you could use ADDR_CLF (ADDRESS in company, last name, first name order). Be sure to enter source type LF in this second screen too.

Start the prompted insertion mode with IP in the left column. The logical file definition is extremely simple. First, select a record type and simply use the name from the physical file (ADDREC). Now you will add one new item to this line: in the function column enter PFILE(ADDRESS). This tells the logical file to reference the physical file named ADDRESS. On the following lines, enter types K (key field) for each of the three keys: COMPANY, LAST, and FIRST. The full definition looks like this:

```
R  ADDREC  PFILE(ADDRESS)
K  COMPANY
K  LAST
K  FIRST
```

That is all there is to it! Now you can save the file and compile it. Because you did not enter any field names, the AS/400 simply copies the field definitions from the physical file defintion in the same order using the same data lengths and functions.

RELATIONAL PROJECT

Now, that last statement may have caught your attention. What would have happened had you entered field names? When fields are defined in a logical file, the view will be restricted to only those named fields, a handy tool for limiting access to sensitive data such as salaries. In relational terminology, column selection is called a *relational project.* Coupled with the AS/400's security provisions, projections (restricted views) work as an effective database management utility.

However, with a logical file, you can do more than simply project fields, you can completely redefine the field attributes. For example, you can designate a field as view-only or input-only. You can change the field width (but bear in mind that a lengthened field will be truncated when written to the physical file), or you can change default entry values and column headings.

DATA TYPES

As a PC user or programmer, you may find some of the AS/400 data types unfamiliar. Most of the preceding examples used A for alphanumeric data types. The data types are:

Code	*Type*	*Length*
A	Alphanumeric	1–32766 fixed or 1–32740 variable
P	Packed Decimal	1–31
S	Zoned Decimal	1–31

Code	*Type*	*Length*
F	Floating Point	1–9 (single precision) or 1–17 (double precision)
L	Date	6, 8, or 10
T	Time	8
Z	Timestamp	26
B	Binary	1–9
H	Hexadecimal	1–32766

For all data types, the length indicates the number of characters in the data: Bytes for alphanumeric and digits for numbers.

The AS/400 was not designed for number crunching. Hence, floating point representation should be avoided. Beyond the performance issue, floating point is not well suited for many of the tasks required of a database; you will find more AS/400s performing financial tasks, rather than scientific tasks.

Floating point representation has rounding problems that can cause unexpected side effects in financial applications. For example, an amount such as $100.01 might be internally represented as $100.00999999...; if you run a query for >=100.01, you might miss some critical data. When precise measurements following a standard format are required (e.g., to the penny), a fixed-point representation is usually preferable.

The AS/400 uses two types of fixed-point representation: Packed decimal and zoned decimal. The length indicates the number of digits in the number. In packed decimal representation the AS/400 always adds 1 byte of storage for the sign (positive or negative); since storage is allocated in even units, you will make more efficient use of system resources if you always use odd sizes. There are other benefits to this approach, which are covered in the next chapter.

RELATIONAL SELECT

In some respects, the DDS can be considered the relational language of the AS/400. It does not have all of the features of a management language such as SQL (structured query language), which is available on the AS/400, but, like a relational language, the DDS can use *relational select*; i.e., a logical file can specify conditions that reduce the number of displayed records, much as project limits the displayed columns or fields.

Thus far, you have seen two formats specified in the name type column of the DDS: "R" for record name and "K" for key. In logical files, you may specify an "S" for the select keyword (note: this is not the same as the relational select operator). With the select keyword, you may enter COMP() in the function column to designate the selection criteria. Consider the address list used in previous examples. If you want to view only those addresses in Minnesota, you could use the following DDS:

```
R  ADDREC   PFILE(ADDRESS)
K  CLINUM
S  STATE    COMP(EQ 'MN')
```

Consider the implications of such an operation from the standpoint of a PC file. If you were designing a database for your sales team, you might assign every sales representative a particular state. Each PC (one for each representative) would store only data for one state. But management might prefer access to all data simultaneously. So, the manager takes all of the sales representative's files and combines them into a single source. Now, all of the data is duplicated (twice as much storage required) and in danger of getting out of date.

Relational select lets you take the opposite approach of combining several small files into one large file and logically, rather than physically, separating the data. Jill still thinks she has her own file and Jack still thinks he has his own, but there is only one large file and the manager, A. Hill, can see the whole picture, and it is continuously maintained as Jack and Jill update to Hill.

LOGICAL JOIN

At the heart of relational database operation is the ability to manage structured files with consistency and simplicity. When a data file structure changes (for example, new fields are added) you would like backward compatibility so you do not need to rewrite existing programs that access the file. With relational project, you can "force" a file with new fields to adhere to an older format. With relational select, you can combine records from files with similar structures and add conditions that extract the old information.

Both project and relational select reduce the viewed data. Another basic operator, *logical join*, increases the data. Join lets you link two or more files through common fields. Consider the ADDRESS and PHONE files—they share a common CLINUM field. The files are in *normalized* form. Had the phone number information been stored in ADDRESS, several (duplicate) phone fields would have been required within ADDRESS. This would have wasted storage space (for single phone numbers) and imposed arbitrary limits (for large clients with more phone numbers than available fields).

Normalization reduces storage overhead, but increases programming overhead. So, why not let the computer handle the overhead? Join denormalizes the data on the fly. A typical application might be a list of parts and suppliers.

TABLE 4.2 PARTS

PARTNO	*DESC*	*QUAN*
001	Widget	2
002	Thingy	3
003	Doodad	10
004	Foobar	7

TABLE 4.3 SUPPLIER

PARTNO	*SUPPNO*
001	0023
001	0067
002	0013
003	0053
003	0083
004	0026
004	0023

PARTS (Table 4.2) would contain a list of part numbers, descriptions, on-hand quantities, etc. SUPPLIER (Table 4.3) would contain a list of part numbers matched to manufacturers and distributors.

A join simply matches the two tables by part number. Another join (between supplier number and a table of vendors) could add specific information about the supplier. For now, consider the simple join between Parts and Supplier in Table 4.4.

TABLE 4.4 Join between Parts and Supplier

PARTNO	*DESC*	*QUAN*	*SUPPNO*
001	Widget	2	0023
001	Widget	2	0067
002	Thingy	3	0013
003	Doodad	10	0053
003	Doodad	10	0083
004	Foobar	7	0026
004	Foobar	7	0023

The logical file DDS for the join specifies the file names with the JFILE function. A pair of functions, JOIN and JFLD, specify the file/field name pairs to use. A logical file join uses more than two physical files, thus it is necessary to designate each separate join as a file/field pair. The DDS for PARTS joined to SUPPLIER (called PARSUP) follows:

```
R  PJSREC           JFILE(PARTS SUPPLIER)
J              JOIN(PARTS SUPPLIER) +
               JFLD(PARTNO PARTNO)
   PARTNO           JREF(PARTS)
   DESC
   QUAN
   SUPPNO
K  PARTNO
```

Note the "+" after the JOIN function. Normally, the JOIN and JFLD functions would appear on a single source line. However, there is not enough room in the function field. The "+" acts as a continuation character to the next line of source code. Also, note the JREF function. Both PARTS and SUPPLIER have a field named PARTNO. The JREF function tells the system which physical file PARTNO references.

MULTIRECORD FORMATS

PC programmers tend to look at storage in a very unstructured manner. A PC's storage space, both memory and disk space, is simply one large chunk of bytes; it is up to the programmer to manage the allocation and data format. For example, consider a simple address file written in a compiled language such as C. The C language uses a struct statement to format data into record-like chunks. Consider a simplified character format for name, address, city, state, and zip code:

```
struct ADDRESS {
   char name[15];
   char address[15];
   char city[10];
   char state[2];
   char zip[5];
} address;
```

Now, what do you do about the phone number? Some people have one phone number, others have many (fax, modem, voice, home, work, etc.). You could add a key field and open another file for phone numbers. Of course, with such an approach, you must write your own relational management routines. If this is supposed to be a quick, simple solution, you would probably write the information to the same file.

Perhaps you would decide to append the phone numbers to the end of the record. You could add a number (integer) called *count* that specifies how many phone numbers follow the address record:

```
struct ADDRESS {
   char name[15];
   char addr[15];
   char city[10];
   char state[3];
   char zip[5];
   int  count;
} address;
```

Now, build a structure for phone numbers. It will be much easier to manage (when reading or writing the file) if the phone number record is the same size as the address record: 50 bytes if the integer allocation is 2 bytes. A phone number might use 15 bytes, so you might as well use the extra space for an extension, if any, and a note (e.g., whether the number is FAX, home, direct, or whatever):

```
struct PHONE {
   char number[13];
   char ext[4];
   char note[33];
} phone;
```

If you are not familiar with C, the variables listed above are addressed by specifying the structure (record) name, a dot, and then the variable (field) name. Thus, the phone number is phone.number and the address is address.addr.

Although you can arbitrarily *cast* (assign) a structure to any memory space in C, there are simpler ways to manage multiple structures in one data area. The C union allows several different formats to share the same memory space.

```
union {
   struct ADDRESS address;
   struct PHONE phone;
} mrf;
```

Now, mrf.address.addr specifies an address and mrf.phone.number specifies a phone number.

Because the AS/400 is a database machine, it organizes storage (files) in a very structured manner. In the preceding C examples, the program structures the data space. If you change the data structures, the file format will change. This can create several problems. For example, files created under the old structure are obsolete and any other programs that rely on the old structure must be modified.

On the AS/400, the data space already has a structure that was defined when you designed the DDS, and the structure is rigidly defined. It simply is not possible to create a physical file that has a "flexible" structure like the C union. At first glance this appears to create new problems. You may feel "locked" into an obsolete format or lose flexibility in your file format definitions. The former problem is resolved with logical file structures you have already seen. Simply create a logical file using the old data format applied to the new physical file definition; the programs need never "know" that they are dealing with logical files rather than physical files.

What you may find surprising is that the AS/400 addresses the second problem, too. Logical files can manage multiple formats in a manner similar to the C union. A logical file that supports two or more record formats is called a multirecord format. Unlike the C programming example, which used a single data space with two separate representations, a multirecord format points to separate data areas (physical files). The two files must share a common indexed (key) field, so the AS/400 knows how to match the records in one file to the records in the other. Consider the ADDRESS file created earlier; it uses a double key of CLINUM and SUBENT. Now you can create a PHONE file that shares at least one field with CLINUM. Either CLINUM or a combination of CLINUM and SUBENT would be the most obvious choices.

```
                    UNIQUE
R   PHONEREC
    CLINUM          10A
    NUMBER          14A
    EXTENSION       4A
    NOTE            20A
K   CLINUM
K   NUMBER
K   EXTENSION
```

You do not need to be concerned with matching record lengths. In C, the union does not require a match either, but managing different record lengths on the PC can be difficult since you must calculate the file offset. Because the AS/400 links the data through a matching key field, it can automatically manage the pointers; all you see is the data you need.

The logical file definition simply links the two physical files on a key, which need not be the same key specified in the physical file definition. The RDEX file combines the record formats from ADDRESS and PHONE, ADDREC and PHONEREC, respectively:

```
R    ADDREC      PFILE(ADDRESS)
K    CLINUM
R    PHONEREC    PFILE(PHONE)
K    CLINUM
```

When a program uses the resulting logical file, the sequential records may follow different formats. For example, the following sequence might appear (to save space, only a few sample fields are shown):

```
1    RSA    ROCHESTER      MN
1    507    288-1644       VOICE
1    507    288-8372       FAX
2    IBM    SOMERS         NY
3    DK     MINNEAPOLIS    MN
3    612    823-7648
```

The first, fourth, and fifth records follow the ADDREC format. The remaining records follow the PHONEREC format. The system manages the overhead of "ordering" the records and changing the record format as needed.

SUMMARY

Unlike the PC environment, which uses a hierarchical storage system, or directory tree, the AS/400 uses single level store, with libraries to organize files. A library list permits users to run files in multiple libraries and affects data files in a manner similar to the DOS command APPEND. Four principle types of libraries are system, user, current, and product. Most libraries fall into the first two categories.

The library list is also handy for application development and database work, for which the AS/400 was designed. To create a database file, first write the source code that describes the file, the DDS (data description specification). Do this with the PDM (Programming Development Manager), which is part of the Application Development Tools package and is the development system of choice for the AS/400. The DDS provides an editor, the SEU (source entry utility) that supports strict formatting conventions and syntax checking. The DFU (data file utility) is designed to assist in data entry.

Although the AS/400 is not fully relational, databases on the systems can be designed to take advantage of many of the features of relational design, including unique key values, views (logical files), relational selection in a database language, and logical joins.

In conclusion, in this chapter you have had an introduction to the AS/400 architecture. You have learned how to build database files and to apply E.F. Codd's relational rules to the AS/400. You have also learned the following commands:

ADDLIBLE	Add a library to the library list
CRTSRCPF	Create a file for physical file source code
CRTLIB	Create a new library
DSPLIBL	Display the library list
EDTLIBL	Edit the user portion of the library list
STRPDM	Start the Program Development Manager

5

Control Language Programming

Controlling the flow of work through a computer is an essential part of any computer system. DOS uses commands to perform a variety of functions that include gaining access to disk files, running programs, and organizing disk space and files by means of directories and subdirectories. Specific applications or tasks often require the use of a series of programs and commands that are repeated each time they are run. DOS uses a construct called a batch file, which is simply a text file that replicates the actions required to perform a task or run an application. You can use your favorite text editor to create and modify a series of instructions in a file and give the file name an extension of .BAT to create a batch file. It is a very simple and useful construct. All you need to do to run this series of instructions is to enter the name of the batch file as you would enter the name of a command.

AS/400 has a similar, but more powerful capability for controlling the flow of work through a system and for managing system functions. It is appropriately named Control Language, or CL. You can use a wealth of commands and create commands of your own, then use of series of these commands in a Command Language program (CLP), which is functionally similar to a DOS batch file.

Suppose you wanted to establish a path that allowed you to run some DOS commands and also some programs named AR01, AR02, and AR03 from a directory named ACCTREC. The files used by these programs are found in directories named ARDAILY, ARWKLY, and ARMONTH. To do this in DOS you might edit a batch file named ARAPP.BAT and add a path command to gain access to the DOS directory and the ACCTREC directory, include an APPEND statement to gain access to the directories with the files, then run the three programs. The batch file might look like this:

```
PATH=C:\DOS;C:\ACCTREC
APPEND C:\ARDAILY;C:\ARWKLY;C:\ARMONTH
AR01
AR02
AR03
```

A CLP to accomplish this same task looks similar to the batch file. Instead of directories, the AS/400 uses libraries. Both files and programs are stored in libraries, but the AS/400 can search through libraries for either files or libraries using a construct called a library list. Consequently, the PATH and APPEND statements are replaced by a single AS/400 command that changes the library list (CHGLIBL); then the programs are called.

```
PGM
CHGLIBL LIBL(ACCTREC ARDAILY ARWKLY ARMONTH)
CALL AR01
CALL AR02
CALL AR03
ENDPGM
```

The PGM and ENDPGM commands at the beginning and end of the CLP are not technically necessary in this case, but programs that receive parameters must have a PGM statement, so using them consistently is a good habit to form. Elementary CLPs are easy to write and are comparable to DOS batch files. There are a few differences you should be aware of, however, and there are other powerful capabilities that are too numerous to cover in this book. We will look at a some of the differences and a few additional capabilities.

When DOS processes a batch file, the command processor must read the text from the batch file and interpret the meaning on the fly, and it must do this each time it runs the batch file. In order to process CLPs more efficiently, the AS/400 compiles CLPs into program objects so that the interpreting step is done only once. Compilation is accomplished by using the CRTCLPGM (create Control Language program) command. Thus setting up a CLP is a two-step process on the AS/400. CLP text (source) is edited in the first step, then created (compiled) from the source in the second step. The Program Development Manager (PDM), described in Chapter 4, provides a means of editing source members and then creating the associated program object. Because this same two-step process is used with all languages on the AS/400, PDM is recommended as an effective way of working with CLP and all of the other programming languages on the AS/400.

Suppose you need to back up the entire contents of the ARDAILY library to a magnetic tape every day. You want to do that at a time when the contents of the library are not in use. You know that the library will not be in use at 2:00 A.M. and that it would be a good time to save the library. Your computer operator does not come to work until 8:30 A.M., however. By that time the data in the library is in use by some remote terminals on the East Coast. The AS/400 has a solution to that problem by allowing you to save a library to a "save file" and by using a job scheduler that can cause a job to run on schedule. At a later time when the operator is available to mount a tape in the tape drive, the "save file" can be copied to magnetic tape. A save file needs to be created to hold the data. After giving this idea a little thought, suppose we realize that ARDAILY is not the only library we would like to back up on a regular basis, so for convenience we decide to create a special library that can contain all the save files. When we do that we can conveniently name the save file the same name as the library that will be saved to it. We decide to name the library ALLSAVE. The library is created via the command:

```
CRTLIB ALLSAVE
```

Next we create the save file named ARDAILY in the ALLSAVE library via the command:

```
CRTSAVF FILE(ALLSAVE/ARDAILY)
```

With those administrative details taken care of we can now concentrate on writing the CLP that will do our daily save operation. We will name our program DAILYSAVE2. We can save the ARDAILY library to the ARDAILY save file via the SAVLIB command, but before we re-use the save file, we need to take care of a minor housekeeping chore; the save file needs to be cleared of its prior day's save contents first. Therefore, the program needs to clear the save file, then save the library to the save file. The program looks like this:

```
PGM
CLRSAVF SAVF(ALLSAVE/ARDAILY)
SAVLIB LIB(ARDAILY) +
   DEV(*SAVF) +
   SAVF(ALLSAVE/ARDAILY) +
   DTACPR(*YES)
ENDPGM
```

The first command, CLRSAVF, clears the save file named ARDAILY in library ALLSAVE. SAVF is the name of the only parameter used in this command, and the value ALLSAVE/ARDAILY is the qualified name of the save file. A qualified name simply means that the library name and file name are separated by a slash. Thus SAVF(ALLSAVE/ARDAILY) is the save file parameter that names the save file that is cleared. The second command, SAVLIB, has four parameters. In this example the command is coded on four lines and a "+" is used to indicate that the command is continued on the next line. A command with multiple parameters can be written on a single line if it will fit. The following command is equivalent to the four lines shown above:

```
SAVLIB LIB(ARDAILY) DEV(*SAVF) SAVF(ALLSAVE/ARDAILY) DTACPR(*YES)
```

The LIB parameter names the library to save. The DEV parameter names the device that receives the saved data. The device name could be the name of a tape drive, a diskette drive, or a special value, *SAVF, to indicate that the save will be directed to a save file rather than an off-line storage device. When the device is *SAVF, then a save file must also be named. The SAVF parameter names the save file. The fourth parameter is optional and specifies whether data compression should be used. In the interest of saving disk storage space, the *YES option was chosen.

This program must be compiled before it can be used. After compilation it is run by calling it via the call command:

```
CALL DAILYSAVE2
```

This simple program makes it easy to save the library to a save file. We began by saying that we wanted to automate this process so that an unattended save could take place at 2:00 A.M. This can be done by using the job scheduling function via the command to work with job schedule entries, WRKJOBSCDE. The command presents a list of scheduled jobs and the ability to add new jobs via the F6 key. Pressing the F6 key to add this job presents a screen into which you enter information that tells how to schedule this job. It asks for a job name, a command to run, the frequency with which the job is run, the day, and the time. Choosing a name for the job, the command to run, and the time is straightforward. We can choose any name such as DAILY. The command is CALL DAILYSAVE2, and the time is 02:00:00 on the 24-hour clock. The choices for frequency and schedule day are slightly confusing at first. To run the job every day of the week, you would choose the value *WEEKLY for frequency and the value *ALL for schedule day. The reason becomes a little less confusing when you understand that to run this job every Monday through Friday you would choose the value *WEEKLY for frequency and multiple values of (*MON *TUE *WED *THU *FRI) for the schedule day.

With this arrangement in place the system operator can take the final step of copying the saved libraries to tape at any time during the day. This is accomplished via the "save save file data" command, SAVSAVFDTA.

```
SAVSAVFDTA SAVF(ALLSAVE/ARDAILY) DEV(TAP01) ENDOPT(*UNLOAD)
```

By now you recognize the first parameter as the name of the save file that is copied to magnetic tape. The DEV parameter names the tape drive on which the tape will be mounted, and the ENDOPT parameter tells the system to rewind and unload the tape at the completion of this operation. If you were planning to copy another save file to the same tape, you would choose a different option, ENDOPT(*LEAVE), which would leave the tape positioned to continue writing more information on it.

Up to this point we have shown how to write a simple program to save a library to a save file, then schedule the save to take place at 2:00 A.M. each day. The operator can then copy the saved library to off-line storage media at some time during the day when it is convenient to work with the tape media.

Suppose that you really want to expand this daily operation to save additional libraries, say GLDAILY, ORDERS, and PAYABLES. One way to do this would be to go back to the original CL program and add a pair of commands (CLRSAVF & SAVLIB) for each additional library. Another approach that illustrates some of the flexibility of the CL language is to modify the original program to accept the name of the library as a parameter and then substitute that parameter name in place of the library name. This can be done by changing the PGM statement to accept a parameter and adding a declare statement (DCL) to the program to define the characteristics of the parameter data. Names, library names included, on the AS/400 can be a maximum of ten characters in length. Consequently, the variable that represents the library name must be a character variable with a length of ten. Parameter names always begin with the "&" character and are immediately followed by a name of up to ten characters. Here is how the program looks after modifying it to accept a library as a parameter value named &LIBNAME.

```
PGM PARM(&LIBNAME)
DCL VAR(&LIBNAME) TYPE(*CHAR) LEN(10)
CLRSAVF SAVF(ALLSAVE/&LIBNAME)
SAVLIB LIB(&LIBNAME) +
   DEV(*SAVF) +
   SAVF(ALLSAVE/&LIBNAME) +
   DTACPR(*YES)
ENDPGM
```

Notice that the PGM statement defines the name of a parameter, the DCL statement defines the data attributes of the parameter, and the commands were changed to use the parameter name instead of ARDAILY, the name of the library. Now to save the additional libraries we need to create the appropriate save files in the ALLSAVE library.

```
CRTSAVF FILE(ALLSAVE/GLDAILY)
CRTSAVF FILE(ALLSAVE/ORDERS)
CRTSAVF FILE(ALLSAVE/PAYABLES)
```

Now we need to call the program four times and pass the appropriate library name each time to save the four libraries to the save files. We can do this with the following calls:

```
CALL DAILYSAVE2 PARM(ARDAILY)
CALL DAILYSAVE2 PARM(GLDAILY)
CALL DAILYSAVE2 PARM(ORDERS)
CALL DAILYSAVE2 PARM(PAYABLES)
```

The first call will do what the original program did: Clear the ARDAILY save file and save the ARDAILY library into the save file. The subsequent calls will clear and then save appropriately as well.

You will recall that our job schedule entry issues a call every morning to DAILYSAVE2, but it does not pass a parameter value. That schedule job will fail because the DAILYSAVE2 program requires a parameter value. We can solve that problem in one of two ways. We could change the scheduled job to issue a parameter and add three more scheduled jobs. The other method is more promising, however. We could make a new program named DAILYSAVE1 that issues the four calls:

```
PGM
CALL DAILYSAVE2 PARM(ARDAILY)
CALL DAILYSAVE2 PARM(GLDAILY)
CALL DAILYSAVE2 PARM(ORDERS)
CALL DAILYSAVE2 PARM(PAYABLES)
ENDPGM
```

Then we could change the job schedule entry to CALL DAILYSAVE1 instead of CALL DAILYSAVE2. With this arrangement, the DAILYSAVE1 program can be modified to save additional libraries by adding calls and passing the name of a library with each call, but do not forget to create the appropriate save file for each save file. But wait, Control Language has a way to automate that as well.

Look at the DAILYSAVE2 program.

```
PGM PARM(&LIBNAME)
DCL VAR(&LIBNAME) TYPE(*CHAR) LEN(10)
CLRSAVF SAVF(ALLSAVE/&LIBNAME)
SAVLIB LIB(&LIBNAME) +
   DEV(*SAVF) +
   SAVF(ALLSAVE/&LIBNAME) +
   DTACPR(*YES)
ENDPGM
```

What would happen if the program received a library name that was invalid? For one thing you probably would not have a save file with that name, and second, the SAVLIB command would fail if by some chance you did have a save file by that name. Fortunately, there is a way to check for the existence of an object (library or save file) before trying to use it. Two facilities in CL are appropriate to resolve this situation. The first is the check object (CHKOBJ) command and the second is the ability to group a series of commands together in a DO group. DO groups start with a DO command and end with an ENDDO command. We will use both of these facilities to resolve this situation.

Before doing the clear and save operations, it seems appropriate to check for the existence of the library we are asked to save. The check object command should therefore be the first executable statement in the program, so it is placed immediately following the declare (DCL) statement and looks like this:

```
CHKOBJ OBJ(QSYS/&LIBNAME) OBJTYPE(*LIB)
```

The name of the object being checked is the library name represented by the variable &LIBNAME and the object type is a library represented by *LIB. The reason we reference QSYS with the library name is that all libraries are referenced through the system library named QSYS; hence the qualified name QSYS/&LIBNAME. The reason for the OBJTYPE parameter is that the CHKOBJ command can check many different kinds of objects such as files (*FILE) or output queues (*OUTQ), so that OBJTYPE(*LIB) is used to specify that we are checking a library object.

How can we determine that the library does not exist after doing the CHKOBJ command? The answer is that the check object command returns messages that indicate the results of the check. The *AS/400 Programming: Reference Summary* SX41-0028 manual, has a section named "Error Messages That Can Be Monitored," which lists each command followed by the possible messages associated with the command. The CHKOBJ command returns up to eight different messages. The one we are interested in is identified by the message ID of CPF9801, which means that the object in question was not found.

MONMSG is the monitor message command that tests for returned messages. In this case, the MONMSG command must immediately follow the CHKOBJ command as shown below:

```
CHKOBJ OBJ(QSYS/&LIBNAME) OBJTYPE(*LIB)
MONMSG MSGID(CPF9801) EXEC(DO)
          .....
          .....
          ENDDO
```

The example above monitors for message ID CPF9801 and if that message is found, then executes the command shown in the EXEC parameter. In this case, we anticipate needing to execute more than one command, so we use the DO command to begin a DO group and end the group with an ENDDO command. We now need to determine what action to take if the library is not found. An appropriate action would be to notify the system operator that the indicated library was not found, then return to the calling program.

```
CHKOBJ OBJ(QSYS/&LIBNAME) OBJTYPE(*LIB)
MONMSG MSGID(CPF9801) EXEC(DO)
      SNDPGMMSG MSGID(UXT2201) +
         MSGF(MSGLIB/ENGMSG) +
         MSGDTA(&LIBNAME) +
         TOMSGQ(*SYSOPR)
      RETURN
      ENDDO
```

The above CLP fragment shows two commands issued as part of the DO group associated with the MONMSG command. A message is sent to the system operator (see the TOMSGQ parameter) and then the program returns to the calling program; in this case, to DAILYSAVE1. You do not have enough information to fully understand the other parameters in the SNDPGMMSG command, so we will not cover that now. The message is sent from a predefined message in a message file. Essentially, we had to create a predefined message with a message number of UXT2201 and place it in a message file named

ENGMSG in library MSGLIB. We also are passing the name of the library as message data (MSGDTA(&LIBNAME)) so that the message facility can insert that library name into the text of the message. Another method of sending a message that is easier to understand, but one that is less helpful, is with the following command:

```
SNDMSG MSG('LIBRARY NOT FOUND') TOMSGQ(*SYSOPR)
```

In this case the message text is included in the message command rather than being taken from a message file, but there is no direct facility in the SNDMSG command to place the name of the library in the text of the message to identify the name of the library. There is an indirect way to do it, but the resulting CLP would not be easy to understand without more knowledge of CLP than you are expected to have at this point.

The CHKOBJ command ensures that the library we are trying to save does in fact exist. The program has not yet ensured that a save file exists to hold the saved library. The CHKOBJ command could be used for this purpose in the following form:

```
CHKOBJ OBJ(ALLSAVE/&LIBNAME) OBJTYPE(*FILE)
MONMSG MSGID(CPF9801) EXEC(DO)
```

An alternative method is to monitor for a message after attempting to clear the save file. Message CPF9812 following a CLRSAVF command indicates that the save file was not found. Programming is simplified somewhat by using this approach. If the save file does not exist, then it should be created. The program below includes the MONMSG and the command to create the needed save file.

```
PGM PARM(&LIBNAME)
DCL VAR(&LIBNAME) TYPE(*CHAR) LEN(10)
CHKOBJ OBJ(QSYS/&LIBNAME) OBJTYPE(*LIB)
MONMSG MSGID(CPF9801) EXEC(DO)
   SNDPGMMSG MSGID(UXT2201) +
      MSGF(MSGLIB/ENGMSG) +
      MSGDTA(&LIBNAME) +
         TOMSGQ(*SYSOPR)
   RETURN
   ENDDO
CLRSAVF SAVF(ALLSAVE/&LIBNAME)
MONMSG MSGID(CPF9812) EXEC(CRTSAVF
```

```
SAVF(ALLSAVE/&LIBNAME))
   SAVLIB LIB(&LIBNAME) +
      DEV(*SAVF) +
      SAVF(ALLSAVE/&LIBNAME) +
      DTACPR(*YES)
   RETURN
   ENDPGM
```

This version of the program tests for the existence of the library that is about to be saved. If the library is not found, the program sends a message and returns to the program DAILYSAVE1 that called it. If the library did exist, then the program makes sure that the save file exists by trying to clear it without checking for its existence. If the file does not exist, then message CPF9812 is detected via the MONMSG command. Because only one command is needed to create the needed save file, it is done directly as the EXEC parameter of the MONMSG command.

There is one library on the AS/400 that should not be backed up via the SAVLIB command. That library is QDOC, which contains document library objects, or DLOs. Control Language has IF-THEN-ELSE logic capability. The IF command is used in the following program fragment to test for QDOC and RETURN to the calling program if an attempt is made to save QDOC with this program.

```
IF COND(&LIBNAME *EQ 'QDOC      ') THEN(RETURN)
```

This command should be inserted immediately following the DCL statement.

An alternative approach that illustrates using a GOTO statement to branch to a label is shown in the following version of the program:

```
PGM PARM(&LIBNAME)
DCL VAR(&LIBNAME) TYPE(*CHAR) LEN(10)
IF COND(&LIBNAME *EQ 'QDOC      ') THEN(GOTO FINAL)
CHKOBJ OBJ(QSYS/&LIBNAME) OBJTYPE(*LIB)
MONMSG MSGID(CPF9801) EXEC(DO)
   SNDPGMMSG MSGID(UXT2201) +
      MSGF(MSGLIB/ENGMSG) +
      MSGDTA(&LIBNAME) +
      TOMSGQ(*SYSOPR)
   RETURN
   ENDDO
CLRSAVF SAVF(ALLSAVE/&LIBNAME)
MONMSG MSGID(CPF9812) EXEC(CRTSAVF
```

```
SAVF(ALLSAVE/&LIBNAME))
   SAVLIB LIB(&LIBNAME) +
      DEV(*SAVF) +
      SAVF(ALLSAVE/&LIBNAME) +
      DTACPR(*YES)
   FINAL:
   RETURN
   ENDPGM
```

The examples have shown some of the most useful features of Control Language programming that can get you started writing useful programs. The following details expand on the examples shown earlier, but should by no means take the place of either further investigation on your own or of formal education.

The examples illustrate how a CLP can receive a single parameter. Two things were required: (1) the parameter variable must be listed in the PARM parameter of the PGM statement and (2) the variable must be defined via a DCL statement. Both conditions must be met for additional parameters as well. The way to specify additional parameters in the PGM statement is shown below:

```
PGM PARM(&FIRST &SECOND &THIRD)
```

Variables used as parameters are coded as a list separated by one or more blanks. The names are prefixed by the "&," which is followed by from one to ten characters for the name. Parameters are passed via a CALL command in a similar fashion.

```
CALL PROGRAM1 PARM(&A &B &C)
```

Parameters need not be named the same in the calling and called programs, but two other rules must be adhered to strictly. The first is that the number of parameters passed and received must be the same. If you attempt to call a program and pass two parameters to a program that expects three parameters, the call will fail. The second rule is that the parameter sequence and data attributes must agree. If the first parameter is a 2000-byte character field, then that is how the field must be defined in both programs. Likewise, numeric (*DEC) variables must be defined with identical lengths and decimal positions, otherwise you will get unpredictable results.

A variable may be declared as any one of three types: *CHAR, *DEC, or *LGL. Character variables TYPE(*CHAR) may have a length ranging from one to a maximum of 9999 characters. Numeric variables are represented internally in packed decimal format of TYPE(*DEC) and may have a maximum of 15 digits with no more than nine digits to the right of the decimal point. Logical variables of TYPE(*LGL) are always one character in length and have a character value of 0 or 1.

The following declares are valid:

```
DCL  VAR(&BIGSTRING) TYPE(*CHAR) LEN(9123)
DCL  &BIGSTRING *CHAR 9123 /* Equivalent to the above */

DCL  VAR(&COUNTER) TYPE(*DEC) LEN(15)
DCL  VAR(&MONEY)   TYPE(*DEC) LEN(7 2)
     /* The variable &MONEY may have a maximum */
               /* value of 99999.99 */
DCL  VAR(&SWITCH) TYPE(*LGL)
DCL  VAR(&ON) TYPE(*LGL) VALUE('1')
DCL  VAR(&OFF) TYPE(*LGL) VALUE('0')
```

The examples used have illustrated some of the very useful features of Control Language programming listed below:

- Passing parameters
- Calling programs from other programs
- Using CHKOBJ to check for the existence of an object
- Using MONMSG to monitor for errors or status conditions
- Use of DO groups
- Use of IF logic
- Use of GOTO and a program label

Control Language is very rich in function, and this brief introduction has only touched on a few of the useful functions by using backup as a practical example of how CLPs can be used. A few words are in order about the structure of commands. You have seen commands used without learning about command grammar. Most commands consist of an implied subject, an action verb, and an object. Some of the verbs used in the earlier examples include:

CRT—Create
CHK—Check
CLR—Clear
MON—Monitor
SAV—Save
SND—Send

Some of the objects in command grammar are:

LIB—Library
MSG—Message
OBJ—Object
PGMMSG—Program message
SAVF—Save file
SAVFDTA—Save file data

Combining verbs and objects yields the commands shown below:

CRTLIB
CHKOBJ
CLRSAVF
MONMSG
SAVLIB
SAVSAVFDTA
SNDMSG
SNDPGMMSG

After learning the available verbs and objects, you can often make an accurate guess about what commands are available. If you want to add a new predefined message to a message file, you might guess that the command is "add message description," or ADDMSGD, and you would be correct. If you had guessed that it was ADDMSGDSC you could use the GO CMDxxx command in the form of GO CMDMSG to get a menu list of all commands that deal with messages and find the command in the list. Where can you find a list of the command verbs and objects? The *AS/400 Programming: Reference Summary*, SX41-0028 manual mentioned earlier has a chapter entitled, "Master CL Command Matrix Table," which lists the commands in a matrix format. That chapter is extremely valuable to experienced programmers and even more valuable for programmers new to CLP. A companion chapter is entitled, "CL Command and Keyword Abbreviations." It lists abbreviations and meanings in alphabetic order by abbreviation.

Working with commands, whether interactively or while editing a Control Language program, is made much simpler by help and prompting capabilities. Help for commands is available on the system by means of the help key F1, and the prompt key F4. You need only key in the command name on a command entry line or while editing a CLP and press the F4 prompt key to see the command with its parameters and a brief description of each parameter. If the brief description is not sufficient, you can place the cursor on the command description and press F1 for more comprehensive help about the command. If you want more help about a parameter, move the cursor to the parameter and press help. If you simply want to know values allowed for a particular parameter, move the cursor to the parameter and press the F4 prompt key. If you are familiar with the keywords associated with parameters and prefer to see the keywords on a prompted command, press F11 when the command is prompted, and the parameter keywords are displayed along with a shortened description of the parameter. This is the prompt screen you see if you type the command SAVLIB and press F4.

```
Save Library (SAVLIB)

Type choices, press Enter.

Library . . . . . . . . . . __________
        + for more values   __________
Device  . . . . . . . . . . __________
        * for more values   __________
        +
```

After keying in the name of the library and the device to which the saved library will be copied, additional prompting will ask for appropriate information based on the device type. If the device named a tape drive, you are asked for information such as a tape volume number and whether the tape should rewind, unload, or be left where it is at the end of the save operation. If the device is a diskette, appropriate information will be requested. If the device is the special value *SAVF, then you will be asked for the name of the save file and the name of the library the save file is in. This additional prompting of values after values are entered on the primary prompt screen is called layered prompting. There are several sources for additional information about CLP. One of these that was mentioned earlier is the *AS/400 Programming: Reference Summary*, SC41-0028 manual. The *AS/400 Programming: Control Language Reference*, SC41-0030 manual, has chapters that describe Control Language syntax, expressions in CL commands, the format of command descriptions, command definition for creating your own commands, and detailed descriptions of each command. The *AS/400 Programming: Control Language Programmer's Guide*, SC41-8077 manual, has a wealth of information, including sample code for many of the topics and situations it addresses. Chapters describe how to write CLP; how to control flow between programs via CALL, TFRCTL, and RETURN commands; advanced topics on special callable modules; how to define messages and work with messages; how to debug programs; and more. The *Control Language Programmer's Guide* is must-read material for the serious Control Language programmer. One other important source of information is contained in the form of sample source programs in a library named QUSRTOOL. The QUSRTOOL library has a wealth of sample code in CLP and other high-level languages that perform significant functions not available through normal system functions. Many programmers have found useful ready-to-compile programs or programs that they can modify to perform specific functions they need. Perhaps more importantly, they have discovered useful programming techniques by studying the code. Do not overlook that gold mine! The QUSRTOOL is installed as an option when you install the system, so if you do not find it on your system, it should be on your installation tapes.

SUMMARY

You have been introduced to a powerful language called Control Language, which is AS/400 specific. The language is intended to provide access to system work flow and management of the AS/400 system. You should not expect to write applications in AS/400, but rather use CL to manage the work flow and program sequence while the application is running. In many respects it provides functions similar to those provided by batch files in DOS, but with many more functions.

6

The Design Aids

Just as a building needs a strong foundation, so do business applications rely on a database foundation. The database is built into the hardware and the operating system on the AS/400. Files are database objects, and these objects are integrated into high-level languages (HLL) and into application development utilities. Because the database is object-oriented and integrated, application development is simplified. More importantly, maintaining applications as the business environment or laws change is much easier and leads to high levels of productivity for application development teams (or individuals). When the database functions on the AS/400 are properly exploited, they are closely linked to information displayed interactively on screens and also to information printed in reports. The data attributes, editing specifications, column headings, and field sizes for all your data are inherited from the database. This relieves the application developer from a lot of tedious clerical work. Fortunately for the application developer, the utilities and high-level languages that constitute the design aids on the AS/400 are integrated into this object-oriented database architecture.

AN OBJECT-ORIENTED APPROACH

Programs written for DOS on a PC treat data for output to the screen and input via the keyboard on a variable-by-variable basis. The program is dedicated to handling one input variable at a time. In contrast, the AS/400 architecture uses a display file object to work with a display screen so that data is handled in blocks that may consist of multiple data items in a screen format. For example, a screen format might display information about a customer that includes the customer name, address, date of last order, and account balance. The screen format may optionally be designed to allow any of that data to be changed, and the changed data returned to the program that displayed it. A program that uses such a display file could use a single statement to output the entire screen, then accept all the data from the screen when the enter key is pressed. All cursor movement within the screen format, protection of constant information, and primitive editing to ensure that numeric data is entered in numeric fields is handled by the system and the display file object. While working with a screen with many input fields on it, the user uses the screen much as a person fills out a paper form with a lead pencil and an eraser. If data entered in one of the fields needs to be changed, the user can move the cursor to the field and change it while the data is still on the screen. The programmer is freed from the responsibility of managing the data on a variable-by-variable basis.

The net result of this object-oriented approach is that programs are written to handle complete blocks (records) of information, whether the information comes from a data file or from a display screen. In cases where display screens are used in a program, the program treats the entire screen format as if it were a data record. Each input or output field in the format carries with it the definition for the field including data attributes. Basic editing, control of whether data is numeric or alphanumeric, maximum field sizes, maximum field values, and allowable values are handled by the display file object. In addition, the applications will be consistent from display screen to display screen. Movement from field to field is controlled by the tab key, the field exit key, or as the result of filling a field. When the display screen format is defined using the Screen Design Aid (SDA) or via Data Description Specifications (DDS) using the Source Entry Utility (SEU), you have some control over the movement from field to field. You can specify that the field exit key is mandatory to move from a particular field, for example. For an application developer coming from the PC environment, this represents a big step forward in productivity.

When all of the related information is filled in on a screen, the entire collection of entered data (from input capable fields on the display) is sent to the program at the same time. This is controlled by the depression of the Enter key. You can optionally send that information with the depression of a function key of your choice. From the AS/400 perspective, a program requests information from a display screen and then the system and the program wait while the workstation operator performs the complete display screen activity (reading the screen and entering data). All of the field movement and primitive data editing is handled by the workstation controller, not by the central processing unit or the program. Only when the Enter key or a defined function key is pressed is the system interrupted, so that the program ends the wait state to begin processing the collection of data from the display screen. When the program receives the data, the program can be sure that numeric information is truly numeric, and that other validation specifications built into the display file object have been enforced. The advantage to the programmer is that much of the clerical work involved in display screen handling is removed from the program definition.

An important advantage to the system with regard to performance in a multiuser environment is that the system offloads many of the screen-handling details to a specialized microprocessor, the workstation controller. Figure 6.1 represents an application that uses data files, display screens, and printers. All of the devices (disk, display, printer) are defined to the application in terms of the

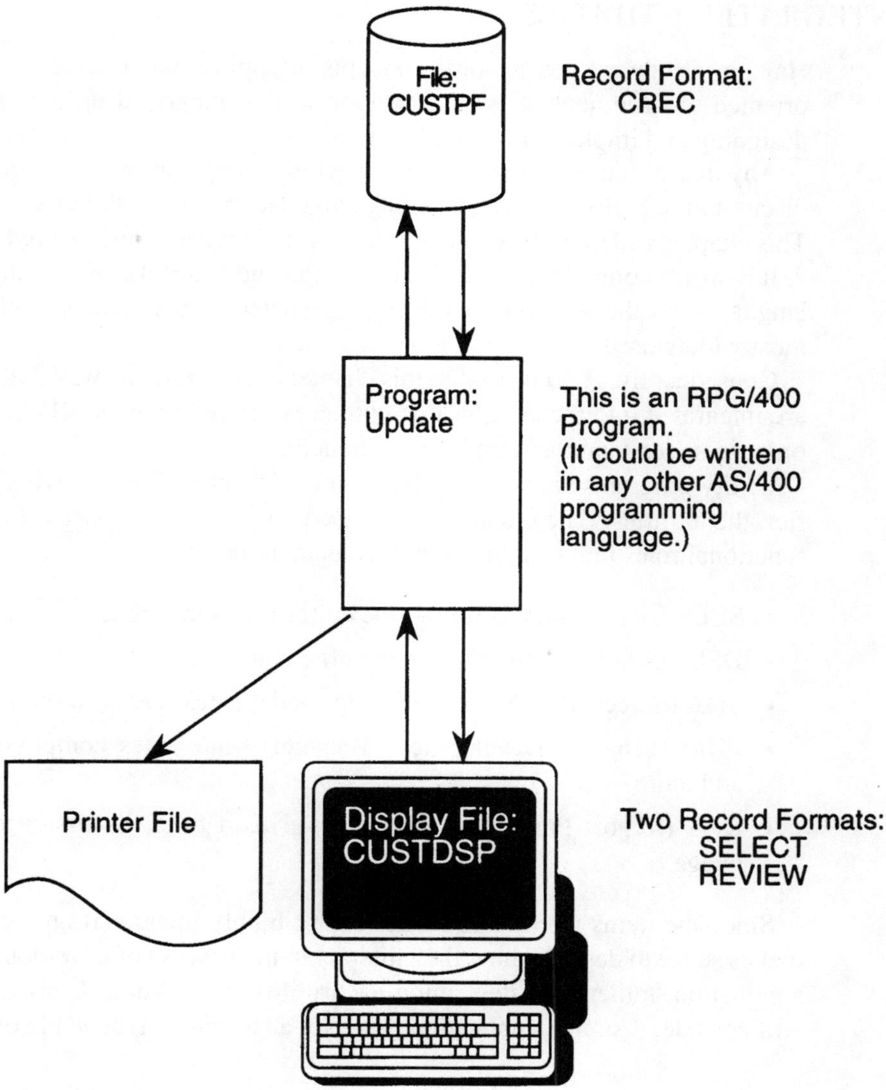

FIGURE 6.1 An application that uses data files, display screens, and printers

input and output data associated with these devices. Thus a printer file definition defines the page size and the exact placement of heading text by specifying the line and column on the page where the first character of the heading is placed. Likewise, all constants and variables are similarly placed by line number and column. Editing of named variables can be based on how the variable is defined in the database. This will be covered in more detail later in the chapter.

INTEGRATED UTILITIES

Having introduced you to some concepts of application structure in an object-oriented environment, it is time to look at the integrated utilities that aid in designing and implementing applications.

Any discussion of design aids for developing applications can hardly avoid a discussion of high-level programming languages and their associated compilers. This chapter will treat the languages lightly, as languages are covered in Chapter 7. It is worth noting that two languages, RPG and COBOL, are the most popular languages on the AS/400 for developing business applications, with RPG the most widely used.

Consequently, RPG is used in this chapter to illustrate the way that languages are integrated into the system. It is not necessary to know the RPG language in order to understand the samples used in here.

Utility programs are the main focus in this chapter. The following list identifies the utilities. They will be described in this chapter according to their functional roles in the application development process.

- SEU (Source Entry Utility)—the editor for source code
- DFU (Data File Utility)—the data file editor
- SDA (Screen Design Aid)—designs and creates screen formats
- PDM (Program Development Manager)—integrates compilers, utilities, and more
- RPG (Report Program Generator)—gives a brief discussion of the language

Since the items mentioned earlier are so highly integrated on the system, it makes sense to describe how they interact in the process of developing a simple application, rather than describing each utility in isolation. Consequently, we will consider a simple application based on an accounts-receivable database.

The database begins with a definition of the information needed in the files. Each account has a name and an address to which monthly statements and correspondence must be routed. Other information pertaining to the account includes such things as the account balance, an account status code, and the name and phone number of the individual who has account responsibility. The database must also contain definitions of the data that describes activity on the account. That might include such things as invoice numbers, transaction date, the invoice amount, payment amounts, and adjustment amounts. Some of this data is used in calculations. Invoice amounts, payments, and adjustments are summed to arrive at an account balance. Other information is used strictly for reference, such as name, zip code, and account number. Clearly, the numeric information that enters into calculations is different from alphabetic and numeric information used for reference. Consequently, the attributes associated with data varies depending upon the intended usage of the data. All of these factors are taken into consideration when a database is defined. A recommended way of establishing a dictionary of all the data used in an application (or even on the entire system) is by means of a reference file. A reference file is a data object that describes each data element (each field) and provides a complete definition of all the attributes associated with each data element.

A partial list of attributes helps to explain what is needed in the reference file.

- Unique name used to identify the data item (field name)
- Alphabetic, numeric, or mixed alphanumeric
- Maximum length of the data (number of characters or digits)
- Number of digits to the right of the decimal point
- Internal representation of computational data
- Text for a column heading associated with the data item

Using the above concepts, information can be represented using the notation shown below. NAME is the field name for the customer's name. The maximum length of the customer name is 25 characters in alphanumeric (alphabetic/numeric mix) representation, indicated by 25A. The column heading is specified via the COLHDG function keyword.

```
ACCTNO        5A             COLHDG('Account' 'Number')
NAME         25A             COLHDG('Customer' 'Name')
ADDR         25A             COLHDG('Street' 'Address')
BAL           7P 2           COLHDG('Account' 'Balance')
```

Given this specification for NAME, the column heading attribute for NAME with a value in the variable of "ABC Construction Company" could appear in any of three orientations: Column, left, or right. Two of these are shown below.

Column Heading orientation:

```
Customer
Name
ABC Construction Company
```

Left orientation:

```
Customer Name: ABC Construction Company
```

Notice that the column heading is shown as two lines because the COLHDG keyword value is defined as two strings of characters. The AS/400 allows a maximum of three lines of heading when used in the columnar orientation. When the heading is oriented to the left or right of the data, the heading information is oriented in a single line, as shown above. Using the column heading information is optional. In some cases you might choose to display or print the information without a heading or you might choose some other heading.

The BAL field differs from the other fields because it is a computed numeric field. In this case, the 7P 2 indicates that the numeric field allows for a maximum of seven digits, two of which are to the right of the decimal point. Thus the digits represented by xs, as in xxxxx.xx, describe the way the data is represented. The P indicates that the data is internally stored as packed decimal numeric data. Packed decimal storage packs two decimal digits in an 8-bit byte except for the low order byte of the field. The low order byte contains a single digit plus the sign of the numeric value. Thus a seven-digit field is stored in 4 bytes, 1 byte for the low order digit and sign with the remaining six digits packed into 3 additional bytes. Because the AS/400 is designed for a commercial environment, this method of representing numeric data avoids the binary round-off errors encountered when dealing with binary floating point data.

The AS/400 uses packed decimal representation of numeric data for computation; therefore, packed decimal representation is the most efficient computational method of representing numeric data. Packed decimal is therefore the default representation, so that if BAL had been defined with a blank space in place of the P, the resulting definition would be the same. Both methods of definition below yield the same result.

```
BAL            7P 2                COLHDG('Account' 'Balance')
BAL            7  2                COLHDG('Account' 'Balance')
```

COLHDG is but one of many function keywords that provide attributes for fields. EDTWRD is a keyword that defines an edit word for numeric data editing. EDTWRD(' $0.   ') specifies the extent of zero suppression and a floating dollar sign. Multiple function keywords can be associated with a single data field. Thus both an edit word and a column heading can be associated with the BAL field as illustrated below:

```
BAL         7  2                   COLHDG('Account' 'Balance')
                                   EDTWRD('     $0.  &CR')
```

The edit word shown above provides the functions described in the earlier paragraph and also causes a blank space followed by "CR" to print following the numeric data if the value is negative; i.e., a credit balance. Thus a credit balance of 12.95 would print as $12.95 CR.

THE SOURCE ENTRY UTILITY

Now that you have had a quick introduction to how Data Description Specifications (DDSs) are structured, it is appropriate to look at the Source Entry Utility (SEU), which is used to edit the specifications for the reference file that will serve as our data dictionary. You may have noticed in the examples that the information is coded in tabular form so that the position of definition data within the line of code is significant. In fact, that is the case, and the SEU not only checks the syntax of the specifications as you enter them, but it also provides a prompted method of entering the specifications so that you do not need to be concerned about the exact positioning within the specification line of source code.

Start the SEU by typing STRSEU on a command line and then pressing the F4 key to prompt for the parameters of the STRSEU command. Figure 6.2 illustrates the appearance of the AS/400 main menu with the command line near the bottom after STRSEU has been typed on the line.

```
          AS/400 Main Menu
Select one of the following:
     1. User Tasks
     2. Office Tasks
     .
     .
     .
     90. Sign off

Selection or command:
===>STRSEU____________________________________________
```

FIGURE 6.2 The AS/400 main menu

Pressing the F4 prompt key brings up the screen in Figure 6.2. Assume that you keep your DDS specifications for the reference file and other files in a source file named QDDSSRC and that the source file is in a library named ARLIB (Accounts Receivable Library). You want to give a name to the reference object. The name can be anything you choose, say DICTIONARY. Figure 6.3 illustrates how you would fill in the prompted parameters on the STRSEU prompt screen.

```
Source file ..........QDDSSRC
Library ..............ARLIB
Source member ........DICTIONARY
Source type ..........PF
Option ...............2
Text description .....This is the A/R Reference file object
```

FIGURE 6.3 The STRSEU prompt screen

Before you go any farther, you should make a note to yourself about how to end this process. On a 3 × 5 card, or other suitable piece of paper, put four x's in the bottom left corner with some small lines like rays emitted from them to represent a flashing error number. To the right of these x's add the following information:

```
F3=Exit                                   F12=Cancel
```

Then label this data with some explanatory comments. Your label for these x's might say, "Press reset, then tab." When you see the flashing number in the lower left corner, press Reset and perhaps press the tab key after Reset. The flashing number in the lower left corner usually is an error code that is hardware determined based on the type and model of workstation being used. It usually means that you pressed a key that was not valid at the time based on the type of screen that was being displayed or the position of the cursor. You will need to reference a specific manual for the particular display to learn the meaning of these error codes.

If you need to back out of an application, F3 or F12 is the most likely choice. Most of the time pressing F3 one or more times will end an application. Sometimes, however, the F3 key is disabled and F12 is used to go back to the previous screen. Consequently, your label for F3 might say, "Exit/Quit," and your label for F12 might say, "Back up one screen." It is important is to take notice of the function keys and the flashing error message to determine the proper approach for backing out of a problem.

In more extreme cases, you may be able to press System Request, then Enter, then take option 2 to end the job or the program that is hung up. On some keyboards, the system request function is activated by pressing a combination of the Alt key plus one other key. You might want to note on the card, "If all else fails, press SysReq, then Enter, and take option 2."

Now that you have created this "quick escape" reference card, put it somewhere near the workstation for handy reference. This reference is good for most AS/400 programs and utilities, not just for SEU alone.

The above values assume that both the library (ARLIB) and the source file (QDDSSRC) exist before this will work. If the library and source file exist and you have the authority to use them, you will see a display that lets you begin entering the DDS for the reference file. It will look something like the sample below in Figure 6.4. The lines with seven apostrophes on the left represent the source data lines. The apostrophes will be automatically replaced by line sequence numbers as you enter source information. If you know the exact format for each DDS line, you could enter that information on the screen without using the prompt facility. For starters you will want to let the prompter guide you through the process. Look at Figure 6.4 and notice the information on the first few lines. The top lines indicate which columns of source data are visible on the display, the name of the member together with the library and source file that the member is in, a SEU command line, and a format line that serves as a guide to the source format.

The SEU command line is used to enter commands that work with the source file. SEU commands let you search for specific character strings, replace one string with another, and perform control functions. Placing the cursor anywhere on the command line and pressing F1 (Help) brings up a description of the commands you can use.

```
Columns . . . :     1  71       Edit                      ARLIB/QDDSSRC
SEU==>______________________________________________________ DICTIONARY
FMT PF.A.....T.Name+++RLen++TDpB...Functions++++++++++++++++++
        ********** Beginning of data ****************************
'''''''
'''''''
'''''''
'''''''
'''''''
'''''''
'''''''
'''''''
'''''''
'''''''
         ****************** End of data ***************************
```

FIGURE 6.4 Entering the DDS for the reference file

The strings of seven apostrophes on the left of each potential line of source code represent sequence numbers. The apostrophes are replaced by sequence numbers when the source lines contain source data. The SEU commands mentioned above are entered on the SEU command line. Other commands, line commands, are issued by typing line commands over the apostrophes or over the sequence numbers that appear to the left of the source data. Prompting for entering source information can be initiated by the use of a line command: P for prompting on a single line and IP to insert and prompt. The IP command prompts for a source line and then prompts for the next one automatically as you finish each source line. A good habit to form when entering line commands is to type the line command followed by a space, then press the enter key to execute the line command. Figure 6.5 shows the line command "IP" followed by a space. The next figure, Figure 6.6, shows the Entry screen with the prompt fields in the lower portion of the screen that is the result of executing the IP line command.

```
 Columns . . . :     1  71      Edit                     ARLIB/QDDSSRC
 SEU==>___________________________________________          DICTIONARY
 FMT PF.A.....T.Name+++RLen++TDpB...Functions+++++++++++++++++
       ********** Beginning of data ***************************
IP ''''
'''''''
'''''''
'''''''
'''''''
'''''''
'''''''
'''''''
'''''''
'''''''
        ****************** End of data **************************
```

FIGURE 6.5 Command "IP" followed by a space

```
Columns . . . :     1  71      Edit                     ARLIB/QDDSSRC
 SEU==>___________________________________________          DICTIONARY
 FMT PF.A.....T.Name+++RLen++TDpB...Functions+++++++++++++++++
       ********** Beginning of data ***************************
'''''''
'''''''
  Prompt type ... PF   Sequence number ... ______

Name                         Data     Decimal
Type     Name      Ref  Length  Type    Positions    Use
 _    __________    _   _____    _         __         _
Functions
_____________________________________________
```

FIGURE 6.6 Result of executing "IP" command

Tip: Place the cursor in an area of the display that you want to know more about and press the help key (F1 or the key labeled Help). In this way you can get a description of line commands when the cursor is in the line sequence number area and help for individual fields on the prompted line when the cursor is in the appropriate prompt field. Cursor-sensitive help is a feature of AS/400 help across all of OS/400, which, of course, is the operating system, and associated utilities.

```
Columns . . . :     1  71       Edit                      ARLIB/QDDSSRC
 SEU==>_____________________________________________________  DICTIONARY
 FMT PF.A.....T.Name+++RLen++TDpB...Functions+++++++++++++++++
       ********** Beginning of data ***************************
'''''''
'''''''
  Prompt type ... PF   Sequence number ... ______

Name                          Data    Decimal
Type     Name      Ref  Length  Type   Positions   Use
 _   NAME______    _   ___25    A        __         _
Functions
COLHDG('Customer' 'Name')___________________
```

FIGURE 6.7 Specifications for the NAME data field

Figure 6.7 illustrates the specifications for the NAME data field as it appears when entered via prompting, and Figure 6.8 shows how it appears in the full screen area after all the prompted data were entered and the Enter key was pressed.

```
Columns . . . :     1  71       Edit                      ARLIB/QDDSSRC
 SEU==>_____________________________________________________  DICTIONARY
 FMT PF.A.....T.Name+++RLen++TDpB...Functions+++++++++++++++++
       ********** Beginning of data ***************************
0001.00 A        NAME        25A      COLHDG('Customer' 'Name')
```

FIGURE 6.8 After NAME data are entered

The only prompted fields that need a value are the name field, the length, data type, and the functions. In a similar fashion the information is entered for ACCTNO, ADDR, and BAL. The information then looks like Figure 6.9.

```
Columns . . . :     1  71       Edit                      ARLIB/QDDSSRC
 SEU==>_____________________________________________________  DICTIONARY
 FMT PF.A.....T.Name+++RLen++TDpB...Functions+++++++++++++++++
       ********** Beginning of data ***************************
0001.00 A        ACCTNO       5A      COLHDG('Account' 'Number')
0002.00 A        NAME        25A      COLHDG('Customer' 'Name')
0003.00 A        ADDR        25A      COLHDG('Street' 'Address')
0004.00 A        BAL          7P 2    COLHDG('Account' 'Balance')
```

FIGURE 6.9 After ACCTNO, ADDR, and BAL data are entered

This completes the data fields for this simple record of four fields, but there is more information needed to complete the record. The record, which is a collection of these four fields, needs a name. Because this record will serve as a reference, let us choose the name "REFREC" as the name of this reference record. In this case, the prompted field labeled "name type" is given a value of R to indicate that this name is a record name and the record name is REFREC. The way to get SEU to prompt for a new line at the top of a source file is to place the IP (insert with prompting) line command on the line above the first sequence number on the left side of the line.

A data dictionary with only four data fields is admittedly of little value, so to be a bit more realistic, the source definition is expanded as illustrated in Figure 6.10.

```
Columns . . . :    1  71      Edit                    ARLIB/QDDSSRC
 SEU==>_____________________________________________      DICTIONARY
 FMT PF.A.....T.Name+++RLen++TDpB...Functions++++++++++++++++++
       ********** Beginning of data ***************************
0001.00 A      R REFREC
0002.00 A        ACCTNO       5A      COLHDG('Account' 'Number')
0003.00 A        NAME        25A      COLHDG('Customer' 'Name')
0004.00 A        ADDR        25A      COLHDG('Street' 'Address')
0005.00 A        CITY        13A      COLHDG('City')
0006.00 A        STATE        2A      COLHDG('State')
0007.00 A        ZIP          5A      COLHDG('Zip' 'Code')
0008.00 A        BAL          7P 2    COLHDG('Account' 'Balance')
0009.00 A                             EDTWRD('     $0.  &CR')
0010.00 A                             TEXT('A computed value')
0011.00 A        DTLP         6S 0    COLHDG('Date of' +
0011.10 A                             'Last Payment')
0012.00 A                             EDTCDE(Y)
0013.00  *     NOTE: An edit code of Y edits a date as mm/dd/yy
0014.00 A        OK           1A      COLHDG('CREDIT' 'OK?')
0015.00 A                             VALUES('Y' 'N')
0016.00 A                             TEXT('Y-good credit, N-no')
0017.00 A        BILCY        2A      COLHDG('Billing' 'Cycle' +
0018.00 A                             'Code')
0019.00 A                             RANGE('01' '20')
0020.00 A        TRDATE       6S 0    COLHDG('Transaction' 'Date')
0021.00 A        TRCODE       1A      COLHDG('Transaction' 'Code')
0022.00 A                             VALUES('1' '2' '3')
0023.00 A                             TEXT('1-Invoice +
0024.00 A                             2-Payment +
0025.00 A                             3-adjust')
0026.00 A        INVC         6A      COLHDG('Invoice' 'Number')
0027.00 A        AMT          7P 2    COLHDG('Transaction' 'Amount')
       ***************** End of data **************************
```

FIGURE 6.10 Expanded source definition

The source definition is complete, but the object has not yet been created. This is analogous to having a source program that has not been compiled into an executable program. Therefore, the next step is to create (compile) the reference file so that we have a reference file object to serve as our data dictionary. The CRTPF (create physical file) command creates the object we need. The CRTPF command needs to know two things, the name of the object it will create and where to find the source that defines the object. To be consistent in naming things, let us choose to name the object DICTIONARY, which is the same name as the source member. Therefore, the object we are about to create will be placed in the library we are using (ARLIB) and will be named DICTIONARY. The source that we just edited is in a member named DICTIONARY, which is a member in the source file named QDDSSRC that exists in library ARLIB. The CRTPF needs to know all of this information in order to create the object and to find the source code that defines the object. You will notice that the AS/400 consistently needs to know the name and location of every object it creates, and it needs to know where to find source definition for objects that are defined by source specifications. You will also notice that all of the create commands begin with the letters CRT. Figure 6.11 illustrates two ways of issuing the CRTPF command. The first, Figure 6.11a, is the prompted form and the second, Figure 6.11b is the unprompted form. Prompting is done by typing the command, CRTPF, on a command line and pressing F4.

```
File...................DICTIONARY
  Library.............  ARLIB
Source file...........QDDSSRC
  Library.............  ARLIB
Source member.........DICTIONARY
   etc.
```

FIGURE 6.11a The prompted form of the CRTPF command

```
CRTPF FILE(ARLIB/DICTIONARY) SRCFILE(ARLIB/QDDSSRC)
            SRCMBR(DICTIONARY)
```

FIGURE 6.11b The unprompted form of the CRTPF command

Notice that the command syntax has three parameters, identified by the keywords FILE, SRCFILE, and SRCMBR. The FILE keyword identifies the parameter that names the object being created. The SRCFILE keyword identifies the source file, and the SRCMBR keyword identifies the source member within the source file. Also notice that the name syntax in the unprompted format remotely resembles the PC DOS path. DOS uses a backward slash as a delimiter, while the AS/400 uses a slash.

```
library-name/object-name    (AS/400)
```

versus

```
directory-name\file-name    (PC DOS)
```

These rather simple steps created a reference file that can be used for a data dictionary.

1. SEU is used to edit the source DDS specifications for a physical file.
2. The physical file (to be used as a data dictionary) is created via the CRTPF command.

That is all it takes to create a file object. It is really quite simple.

PROGRAM DEVELOPMENT MANAGER

A utility that brings together the editor, create commands (compilers), and other utilities is the Program Development Manager. The PDM utility allows access to all of these functions so that in the preceding steps we could have started PDM, then edited using SEU by selecting a PDM option in place of the STRSEU command. After concluding the editing, option 14 compiles the DICTIONARY file in place of the CRTPF command.

Figure 6.12 shows how to start PDM (the STRPDM command) from the MAIN menu.

```
MAIN                      AS/400 Main Menu

 Select one of the following:

      1. User tasks
      2. Office tasks
      3. General system tasks
      4. Files, libraries, and folders
      5. Programming
      6. Communications
      7. Define or change the system
      8. Problem handling
      9. Display a menu
     10. User support and education
     11. PC Support tasks
      .
      .
      .
     90. Sign off

 Selection or command
 ===> STRPDM_______________________________________________

 F3=Exit   F4=Prompt  F9=Retrieve  F12=Cancel  F13=User support
 F23=Set initial menu
```

FIGURE 6.12 Starting PDM from the MAIN menu

The STRPDM command displays the initial PDM menu. The menu shown in Figure 6.13 has four options to choose from. Since we wish to work with source information that is stored in members, we choose option 3 to work with members.

```
        AS/400 Programming Development Manager (PDM)

 Select one of the following:

      1. Work with libraries
      2. Work with objects
      3. Work with members
      .
      .
      .
      9. Work with user-defined options



    Selection or command
 ===> 3_______________________________________________________

 F3=Exit         F4=Prompt       F9=Retrieve      F10=Command entry
 F12=Cancel      F18=Change defaults
```

FIGURE 6.13 PDM menu

The resulting screen lets you specify which members you want to work with. This is done by naming the source file and identifying the name of the library the source file is in, as shown in Figure 6.14. The file is QDDSSRC, found in the library named ARLIB.

```
                     Specify Members to Work With

 Type choices, press Enter.

   File . . . . . . . . . .    QDDSSRC      Name, F4 for list

     Library . . . . . . . .     ARLIB      *LIBL, *CURLIB, name

   Member:
     Name  . . . . . . . . .   *ALL         *ALL, name, *generic*
     Type  . . . . . . . . .   *ALL         *ALL, type, *generic*
```

FIGURE 6.14 Namimg the source file

The next screen displays a list of all members in the selected source file. The following figure (Figure 6.15) displays that list. Since the source file contains only one source member at this point, the only one shown is the member named DICTIONARY.

```
                         Work with Members Using PDM

File  . . . . . .   QDDSSRC
  Library . . . .     ARLIB          Position to ..__________

Type options, press Enter.
  2=Edit        3=Copy     4=Delete      5=Display    6=Print
  7=Rename      8=Display description    9=Save    13=Change text

Opt  Member       Type      Text
2    DICTIONARY   PF        Data Dictionary (Record name REFREC)

Parameters or command
===>__________________________________________________

F3=Exit      F4=Prompt           F5=Refresh         F6=Create
F9=Retrieve  F10=Command entry   F23=More options   F24=More keys
```

FIGURE 6.15 All members in a selected source file

The options are shown above the member name. Option 2 is the choice for editing and causes SEU to edit the member named DICTIONARY. The result is shown back in Figure 6.10, which is identical to what would be displayed if the STRSEU command had been issued to edit the DICTIONARY member.

The preceding example illustrates how PDM can initiate the SEU utility. PDM serves as a pathway to the editor, compilers, and other utility functions. In an earlier step, the DICTIONARY reference file was created using the CRTPF command. The way to create it using the PDM interface is by using option 14, the compile (create) option. Figure 6.16 shows the display screen as it appears after F23 was pressed to cause additional options to be displayed. Notice that the first options shown is option 14=Compile. That option is used alongside the DICTIONARY member to perform the CRTPFM command. If the prompt key, F4, is pressed after entering the 14 option, the prompt for CRTPF is displayed with the information filled in to identify the object and identify the source member that contains the source definition for the file. If the enter key is pressed instead of F4, then the command is submitted without showing the prompted values.

```
                         Work with Members Using PDM

File  . . . . . .    QDDSSRC
  Library . . . .      ARLIB          Position to ... ___________

Type options, press Enter.
  14=Compile              16=Run procedure         17=Change using SDA
  19=Change using RLU     25=Find string ...

Opt  Member       Type       Text
14    DICTIONARY  PF         Data Dictionary (Record name REFREC)

Parameters or command
===>_______________________________________________________
F3=Exit        F4=Prompt          F5=Refresh         F6=Create
F9=Retrieve    F10=Command entry  F23=More options   F24=More keys
```

FIGURE 6.16 Additional options

Now that PDM has been introduced as a pathway to editing source and creating associated objects, it will be used in the remaining examples to illustrate the process of creating a physical file for the customer master file. The first step is to define the customer master file. Because a data dictionary file, DICTIONARY, exists, it will be used to define the data attributes of the data fields in the customer master file. The customer master file is named CUSTPF. Pressing F6 opens a screen allowing a member name, CUSTPF, to be provided along with other information needed for the new source member named CUSTPF.

By specifying the name of the DICTIONARY file as the reference file at the beginning of the source definition for CUSTPF, it becomes easy to select the fields from that reference file to be incorporated into the customer master file. Simply naming the field from the reference file and using an "R" to indicate that the field is to be defined based on the reference file is sufficient to define the field with all of the attributes specified in the reference file. Thus the file definition consists of the REF function keyword to identify the reference file in line sequence 0001.00, a record name source line to name the record in line sequence 0002.00, and a single source line for each field in the CUSTPF file. To finish up the file definition, a source line identifies the field from the record that will serve as the index key to the file. In this case, the last source line shown in Figure 6.17 identifies the key via the "K" followed by the field name NAME in line sequence 0013.00.

```
Columns . . . :    1  71          Edit                 ARLIB/QDDSSRC
 SEU==>_____________________________________________            CUSTPF
 FMT PF .....A..........T.Name++++++RLen++TDpB......Functions++++++++++++
        *************** Beginning of data ***********************
0001.00    A                                    REF(ARLIB/DICTIONARY)
0002.00    A          R CREC
0003.00    A            ACCTNO    R
0004.00    A            NAME      R
0005.00    A            ADDR      R
0006.00    A            CITY      R
0007.00    A            STATE     R
0008.00    A            ZIP       R
0009.00    A            BILCY     R
0010.00    A            BAL       R
0011.00    A            OK        R
0012.00    A            DTLP      R
0013.00    A          K NAME
        ************** End of data ******************************




  F3=Exit   F4=Prompt    F5=Refresh   F9=Retrieve    F10=Cursor
  F16=Repeat find        F17=Repeat change           F24=More keys
```

FIGURE 6.17 Identifying the index key

The next step is to create the CUSTPF file. Once again it is done via option 14, as shown in Figure 6.18.

```
                          Work with Members Using PDM

File  . . . . . .   QDDSSRC
  Library . . . .     ARLIB        Position to ...______________

Type options, press Enter.
  14=Compile              16=Run procedure       17=Change using SDA
  19=Change using RLU   25=Find string ...

Opt  Member      Type     Text
14   CUSTPF      PF       Customer Physical File (
__   DICTIONARY  PF       Data Dictionary (Record name REFREC)



Parameters or command
===>________________________________________________________
F3=Exit       F4=Prompt           F5=Refresh         F6=Create
F9=Retrieve   F10=Command entry   F23=More options   F24=More keys
+
```

FIGURE 6.18 Creating the CUSTPF file

The resulting customer master file has no records in the file, but the definition is complete and ready to receive records.

SCREEN DESIGN AID

The objective is to design a workstation screen that prompts us to enter a customer name that we want to work with, then design a second screen with the information related to the selected customer. The first screen, asking for a customer name, is shown in Figure 6.19.

```
        Customer Information Display

   Select the customer by entering the customer's name


     _________________________  Customer Name
```

FIGURE 6.19 Asking for customer name

Designing the layout of a screen is a little more involved than defining a physical file. Fields need to be placed in two dimensions in a limited amount of space. The Screen Design Aid helps to simplify the design process. There are several ways to begin the process, but the one described in the following scenario makes use of PDM's pathway to SDA. In order for PDM to initiate SDA, a display file source member is needed. Create a source member that has nothing more in it than a single source line naming a record. Then select it for SDA via option 17. The objective is to design two screen formats associated with a single display file.

The first screen is designed to ask the operator to identify the customer by name, after which an associated program will display information about the customer using the second screen format. The second screen format will also allow the operator to make changes to the customer information. Consequently, the simple source member created as a "starter" member contains only one record name, SELECT, which is the name of the record format that will be used to ask the operator to enter the customer name. Figure 6.20 illustrates the definition of the simple starter member, then shows how to select it to design the first format. The figure has been simplified to show only the most significant information.

```
Columns . . . : 1  71        Edit                    ARLIB/QDDSSRC
 SEU==>________________________________________________  CUSTDSP
 FMT DP .....AAN01N02N03T.Name++++++RLen++TDpBLinPosFunctions++++++++++
        *************** Beginning of data ***********************
'''''''    A        R SELECT
'''''''
'''''''
'''''''
'''''''
        ************** End of data *************************
```

FIGURE 6.20 Definition of the simple starter member

Press F3 to end the edit session with the single source statement shown above, then select this new member for SDA using option 17 as shown in Figure 6.21.

```
                        Work with Members Using PDM

 File  . . . . . .    QDDSSRC
   Library . . . .      ARLIB        Position to...________

 Type options, press Enter.
   14=Compile         16=Run procedure       17=Change using SDA
   19=Change using RLU   25=Find string ...

 Opt  Member        Type       Text
 17   CUSTDSP       DSPF       Customer Information Display
      CUSTPF        PF         Customer Physical File (
      DICTIONARY    PF         Data Dictionary (Record name REFREC)
```

FIGURE 6.21 Selecting a new member

Taking option 17 for the member CUSTDSP initiates the SDA menu shown in Figure 6.22. The menu presents a screen from which the designer can choose to work with any available screen format or add new screen formats to the list of formats associated with the display file being designed. Figure 6.22 shows only one format name SELECT. This the name of the starter record name that was created earlier.

```
                      Work with Display Records

File . . . . . . . :    QDDSSRC       Member . . . :    CUSTDSP
  Library . . . . :      ARLIB        Source type  . . . :    DSPF

Type options, press Enter.
  1=Add          2=Edit comments        3=Copy          4=Delete
  7=Rename       8=Select keywords     12=Design image

Opt  Order     Record        Type       Related Subfile    Date
12       10    SELECT        RECORD                        10/17/92



F3=Exit                           F12=Cancel  F14=File-level keywords
F15=File-level comments           F17=Subset  F24=More keys
```

FIGURE 6.22 Initiating the SDA menu

Among the available options is option 12, which is used to design the screen format image. Selecting option 12 causes a nearly empty screen to be displayed. This should not come as a surprise, as the only information in the starter source member consisted of nothing more than a record name, which is the name of the screen format. The only information is an information line at the bottom of the screen that informs the designer of the name of the format plus a "helpful" note informing the designer that the help key, F1, is available for use. The name of the format, SELECT, is displayed at the bottom of the screen.

This empty display screen provides a work space in which to design the SELECT screen format. Placing constant information in this format guides the user. This select screen tells the user to enter a customer name to identify the customer with which to work. Consequently, the constant information must so inform the user and the screen must provide a variable field into which the user can enter the customer name. Figure 6.23 represents one way of designing the screen by typing in the constant textual information enclosed in apostrophes. After the constant text strings have been placed, they are moved to improve the appearance of the screen. Then the input capable variable field into which the customer name will be entered is added by referencing the reference file, DICTIONARY. This will accurately define the attributes of the input capable field.

Since it is known at the outset that the customer name will be entered to identify the customer, one approach is to make that customer name definition available to the screen format that is being designed. Pressing the help key informs the designer that F10 can be pressed to begin the process of selecting the data definitions used in this screen. The designer is interested in only one field, NAME, which is defined in the reference file named DICTIONARY. Consequently that selection is made after pressing F10. Figure 6.23 illustrates the selection process.

```
                         Select Database Files

Type options and names, press Enter.
  1=Display database field list
  2=Select all fields for input (I)
  3=Select all fields for output (O)
  4=Select all fields for both (B) input and output

Option     Database File   Library      Record
  1          DICTIONARY    ARLIB        REFREC


F3=Exit      F4=Prompt     F12=Cancel
```

FIGURE 6.23 Selection process

After the file is selected, another selection screen presents the names of the fields that are available from the reference file. The designer is interested only in the customer name field named NAME and the field to be used for input. An input field is one the user enters information into and that then becomes "input" to the program that reads the screen. Figure 6.24 shows that option 2 placed alongside the NAME field selects it for input.

```
                         Select Database Fields

Record . . . :    REFREC

Type information, press Enter.
  Number of fields to roll  . . . . . . . . . . . . . .        8
  Name of field to search for . . . . . . . . . . . . ________

Type options, press Enter.
  1=Display extended field description
  2=Select for input (I), 3=Select for output (O), 4=Select for both (B)

Option  Field          Length   Type    Column Heading
 __     ACCTNO              5     A     Account Number
 _2     NAME               25     A     Customer Name
 __     ADDR               25     A     Street Address
 __     CITY               13     A     City
 __     STATE               2     A     State
 __     ZIP                 5     A     Zip Code
 __     BAL               7,2     P     Account Balance
 __     DTLP              6,0     S     Date of Last Payment
 __     OK                  1     A     CREDIT OK?

F3=Exit   F12=Cancel
```

FIGURE 6.24 Selecting the NAME field for input

After the selection is made, the empty screen is redisplayed. The bottom line of the display now identifies the selected field by a number and its name, as shown in Figure 6.25. The designer begins to design the screen by ignoring the NAME field while first entering constant textual information to guide the user. The first constant text states the purpose of this display via the string 'Customer Information Display'. Notice that the string is enclosed in apostrophes. The apostrophes are placed there to identify the string to the SDA. The apostrophes disappear when Enter is pressed and are not part of the final screen design. The first apostrophe is replaced by an attribute byte that defines the characteristics of the field (constant string) to the display file. The attribute byte is not visible on the screen. By knowing of its existence, however, the designer can use it to move the entire string to a new place on the screen image.

```
          'Customer Information Display'






 1:NAME
```

FIGURE 6.25 Entering a constant text string

The designer in this example pressed the Enter key after entering the first line of textual constant information, then entered a second line that requests an action by the user. Notice again that the line of text is enclosed in apostrophes. What the designer wants in that line of text is to ask the user to enter the customer's name. Unfortunately, the word "customer's" has an apostrophe in it, which is used for another purpose by SDA. A quick and easy way around that small problem is to use some other character, in this case a minus, and then type over it to replace it after the string has been defined (Figure 6.26).

```
           Customer Information Display

         'Select the customer by entering the customer-s name'





 1:NAME
```

FIGURE 6.26 Replacing the apostrophe with a minus sign

The designer replaced the minus with an apostrophe after the Enter key was pressed to define the second line of text (Figure 6.27). It should be noted here that this example shows placing each line separately and pressing Enter. The designer could have placed all text lines on the screen at the same time before pressing the Enter key to define them.

```
          Customer Information Display

         Select the customer by entering the customer's name






 1:NAME
```

FIGURE 6.27 Replacing the minus sign with an apostrophe

The next step the designer of the screen took was to place the input capable field on the screen. This was done by noting that NAME is identified by the number 1 at the bottom of the work screen (1:NAME). Positioning of referenced fields is accomplished by fixing their position on the screen via an ampersand (&), followed by the reference number associated with the field. Consequently, &1 locates the field on the screen. This positioning identifier can optionally be followed by a code that defines the placement of column heading information. In this case the designer used an r to place the column heading information to the right of the input capable field (Figure 6.28).

```
          Customer Information Display

         Select the customer by entering the customer's name


       &1r






 1:NAME
```

FIGURE 6.28 Placing the input-capable field on screen

Before looking at Figure 6.29, notice that the placement of the first two lines of textual information is not necessarily pleasing to the eye. The lines can be moved easily. That is illustrated in Figure 6.29. Notice also the effect of placing the &1r on the screen and pressing Enter. Remember the COLHDG function keyword used to define the NAME field? Notice how that two-line column heading becomes a single-line "heading" placed to the right of the NAME field.

```
         Customer Information Display

<<<<<<<Select the customer by entering the customer's name


      IIIIIIIIIIIIIIIIIIIIIIII  Customer Name
```

FIGURE 6.29 Two-line column heading is placed to the right of the NAME field

Apparently the designer did not like the positioning of the second line of text after seeing where the input capable field and its associated heading were placed, so the designer moved it by using the < symbol as arrows to move it. Notice that the < symbol must be placed over the invisible attribute byte in order to accomplish the move. The following figure (Figure 6.30) shows the results of the move. Also notice that the field where the customer name can be entered as an input field is identified by a string of "I"s.

```
         Customer Information Display

Select the customer by entering the customer's name


      IIIIIIIIIIIIIIIIIIIIIIII  Customer Name
```

FIGURE 6.30 Results of moving second line of text

This simple SELECT screen format illustrates some of the key elements involved in designing display files. A display file can consist of multiple-screen formats; this example has shown only one so far. A second format is added in later steps. It is worth mentioning now that the example shown above illustrated moving single fields. SDA has facilities for moving larger blocks of screen information by framing a block with a minus sign in the upper left corner of the block and in the lower right corner. An equal sign serves as a target for the upper left corner of the block. Thus large portions of the screen can be relocated easily.

A good practical screen design would include additional information such as a description of the valid function keys and their usage. Just to keep things simple, however, assume that the format design is complete. The designer ends the design of this format by pressing F3. The resulting screen and those that follow it tell what to do to accept the design up to this point. The designer followed those instructions until the "Work with Display Records" menu appeared, as illustrated in the next figure, Figure 6.31. This menu is used to add a new record format. On the blank for the first option, the designer entered option 1 to add a format and typed the format name, REVIEW, in the record column and pressed Enter. Additional information is requested regarding the format and once again a blank screen is displayed at the beginning of the design phase for the SELECT format.

Following the same approach for this format, F10 can be used to select the DICTIONARY file as a reference file and then to select from it the fields to be displayed on the REVIEW screen format. Because the REVIEW screen format displays the data from the customer record and then allows changes to be made, the fields will be used as both output (to display existing data) and input (to type over the data to change it) so that the changed data is input to the program that works with the customer file.

```
              Work with Display Records

File  . . . . :   QDDSSRC         Member . . . . . . :   CUSTDSP
  Library . . :     ARLIB            Source type  . . . :    DSPF

Type options, press Enter.
  1=Add          2=Edit comments     3=Copy           4=Delete
  7=Rename       8=Select keywords   12=Design image

Opt  Order     Record        Type       Related Subfile   Date
1              REVIEW
         10    SELECT        RECORD                       10/17/92
```

FIGURE 6.31 Fields used as both input and output

Adding a new record format, REVIEW, opens a blank screen. The REVIEW screen is defined in the same way as the SELECT screen was designed. F10 is the key that allows selection of predefined data from either a database file or from a reference file to be used on this screen. Just as in the SELECT screen, the DICTIONARY reference file is selected (Figure 6.32).

```
                        Select Database Files

Type options and names, press Enter.
  1=Display database field list
  2=Select all fields for input (I)
  3=Select all fields for output (O)
  4=Select all fields for both (B) input and output

Option     Database File    Library       Record
  1          DICTIONARY     ARLIB         REFREC





F3=Exit      F4=Prompt      F12=Cancel
```

FIGURE 6.32 Selecting the DICTIONARY reference file

After you select the file, select the fields from the file that will be used on the screen format. In this case the fields will both be displayed and changed. Therefore they are selected with option 4, which allows both output and input of the field data (Figure 6.33).

```
                         Select Database Fields

Record . . . :    REFREC

Type information, press Enter.
  Number of fields to roll  . . . . . . . . . . . . . . . . 8
  Name of field to search for . . . . . . . . . .   .__________

Type options, press Enter.
  1=Display extended field description
  2=Select for input (I), 3=Select for output (O), 4=Select for both (B)

Option  Field        Length   Type    Column Heading
  4     NAME             25     A     Customer Name
        ADDR             25     A     Street Address
  4     CITY             13     A     City
  4     STATE             2     A     State
        ZIP               5     A     Zip Code
  4     BAL             7,2     P     Account Balance
  4     DTLP            6,0     S     Date of Last Payment
  4     OK                1     A     CREDIT OK?

More...
 F3=Exit   F12=Cancel
```

FIGURE 6.33 Fields are displayed and changed

After the selection is made, the blank screen returns with the selected fields shown on the last line of the otherwise blank screen. Each field is given a unique number in the format of n:field-name as shown in Figure 6.34.

```
1:NAME 2:CITY 3:STATE 4:BAL 5:DTLP 6:OK
```

FIGURE 6.34 Selected fields are shown on last line

Screen design can proceed, as with the SELECT screen format. Sometimes, however, it is convenient to see another screen image on the format that is being designed. In this case, we would like to see the SELECT screen format while designing the REVIEW screen format. This can be done by asking SDA to display an additional format. Pressing F9 prompts for selection of the additional format (Record) to be displayed. Selecting the SELECT record causes the SELECT format to be displayed along with whatever is being designed on the REVIEW screen format (Figure 6.35).

```
                    Select Additional Records for Display

File . . . . . . :    QDDSSRC               Member . . . . . . :    CUSTDSP
  Library . . . . :     ARLIB               Source type  . . . :    DSPF

Type options, press Enter.
  1,2,3=Select for display as additional record

Option    Record          Type     Status
  1
  2
  3
  1       SELECT          RECORD
          REVIEW          RECORD   In use




F3=Exit      F5=Refresh      F12=Cancel
```

FIGURE 6.35 Selecting the SELECT record

After selecting the additional display, information is displayed as shown in Figure 6.36. That additional information can be toggled to display or can be removed from the display by using F21 as a toggle switch.

```
          Customer Information Display

    Select the customer by entering the customer's name


         IIIIIIIIIIIIIIIIIIIIIIIII  Customer Name






  1:NAME 2:CITY 3:STATE 4:BAL 5:DTLP 6:OK
```

FIGURE 6.36 Results of selecting additional information

While viewing the REVIEW screen with the SELECT screen format superimposed upon it, the fields identified on the last line of the screen can be positioned on this new format. Multiple fields can be requested as shown in Figure 6.37. The "&2," "&3," and "&4" represent the fields CITY, STATE, and BAL. The "R" that follows "&4" indicates that the column heading information associated with the BAL field is to be placed to the right of the data.

```
          Customer Information Display

    Select the customer by entering the customer's name


         IIIIIIIIIIIIIIIIIIIIIIIII  Customer Name

         &2                   &3

         &4R





  1:NAME 2:CITY 3:STATE 4:BAL 5:DTLP 6:OK
```

FIGURE 6.37 Requesting multiple fields

Pressing the enter key processes the information (Figure 6.37) to give a new screen shown in Figure 6.38).

```
          Customer Information Display

   Select the customer by entering the customer's name


        IIIIIIIIIIIIIIIIIIIIIIIIII  Customer Name

        BBBBBBBBBBBBBBBBBBBBBBBBBB

        $99999.99 CR  Account Balance



           &3C                  &2C




1:NAME 2:DTLP 3:OK
```

FIGURE 6.38 Results of requesting additional fields

Additional fields for OK and DTLP are positioned on the screen with a request for heading information in a columnar orientation via the "&3C" and "&2C" entries on the screen. Notice that the fields previously selected from the bottom of the screen are removed from this screen and the remaining fields were renumbered so that 3 and 2 refer to the fields OK and DTLP, respectively (Figure 6.38).

In addition to the changes just made to the screen, the designer wants to redisplay the customer name as both an output and input field so that changes can be made to the customer name. Consequently, an "&1R" is typed directly over the name field. SDA treats the NAME field as if it is not really there because it is part of the added record named SELECT (Figure 6.39).

```
          Customer Information Display

   Select the customer by entering the customer's name


        &1R IIIIIIIIIIIIIIIIIIIII  Customer Name

        BBBBBBBBBBBBBBBBBBBBBBBBB

        $99999.99 CR  Account Balance


           CREDIT               Date of
           OK?             Last Payment
           B                   99/99/99




 1:NAME
```

FIGURE 6.39 Redisplaying the customer name as an input and output field

The results are shown in Figure 6.40. The F21 key can be used to toggle the additional record display on and off so that the REVIEW format can be seen by itself or in combination with the SELECT format. Notice that the customer name field is shown as a string of 25 "B"s because it is a 25-character field that is now defined as both input and output.

Note also that even though the "B"s occupy the same position on the screen that was occupied by "I"s from the SELECT format, the SELECT format was not affected in any way. If we were to go back and look at the SELECT format it would show "I"s for input. Thus when a program uses this display file with these two formats (SELECT and REVIEW), the program will use the SELECT format to request the customer that is to be reviewed. After retrieving the customer information, the REVIEW format will be used to display the customer information and also to change the displayed information in place on the display screen. Consequently, the customer name will appear in the same spot on both screens, but the data attribute of the field will be input on the SELECT screen and both output and input on the REVIEW screen.

```
        Customer Information Display

    Select the customer by entering the customer's name


         BBBBBBBBBBBBBBBBBBBBBBBBB  Customer Name

         BBBBBBBBBBBBB       BB

         $99999.99 CR  Account Balance

            CREDIT                Date of
            OK?              Last Payment
            B                    99/99/99
```

FIGURE 6.40 REVIEW format

The preceding simple steps illustrate the powerful facilities available to the application designer when designing screen formats with the Screen Design Aid, together with a reference file.

A few more steps illustrate how the REVIEW screen can be completed. Pressing F21 removes the SELECT screen format from the view. Next, add a line that says "Review the Customer Information" to identify the REVIEW format visually. Near the bottom of the screen add a line that says "Press F3 to end the job." (See Figure 6.41.)

```
          'Review the Customer Information'


         BBBBBBBBBBBBBBBBBBBBBBBBB  Customer Name

         BBBBBBBBBBBBB       BB

         $99999.99 CR  Account Balance


            CREDIT                Date of
            OK?              Last Payment
            B                    99/99/99


              'Press F3 to end the job'
```

FIGURE 6.41 Completing the REVIEW screen

One remaining item is to provide a way for the display file to tell the program that F3 was pressed so that the program can end gracefully; that can be done at the file level so that F3 will be activated and detected from either format, SELECT or REVIEW. First exit the design of the REVIEW format via the F3 key. The display file communicates the fact that a function key was pressed by turning on an indicator. We will use the keyword CA03 to identify that F3 was pressed and then to turn on an indicator. Any one of 99 indicators from 01–99 can be used for this purpose. Some installations prefer to use indicators that match the function key; for example, CA03 would turn on indicator 03. That may be a good practice to follow, but for this illustration we will turn on indicator 99 to avoid leaving the impression that the function key number must match the indicator number.

Figure 6.42 shows the screen from which file keywords are selected. Note that F14 is the way to start this process.

```
                    Work with Display Records

File . . . . . . :     QDDSSRC              Member . . . . . . :    CUSTDSP
  Library . . . . :      ARLIB              Source type  . . . :    DSPF

Type options, press Enter.
  1=Add              2=Edit comments            3=Copy           4=Delete
  7=Rename           8=Select keywords         12=Design image

Opt  Order     Record     Type     Related Subfile   Date            DDS Error

        10     SELECT     RECORD                     10/17/92
        20     REVIEW     RECORD                     10/17/92


F3=Exit                       F12=Cancel      F14=File-level keywords
F15=File-level comments       F17=Subset      F24=More keys
Record REVIEW added to member CUSTDSP.
```

FIGURE 6.42 Selecting file keywords

After pressing F14, two more displays are needed to finish the specification of the F3 key. The first of these requires a choice among the many different kinds of file level keywords. Indicator keywords is the correct choice (Figure 6.43).

```
                           Select File Keywords

 Member . . . :    CUSTDSP

 Type choices, press Enter.

                                         Y=Yes
   General keywords  . . . . . . . .
   Indicator keywords  . . . . . . .       Y
   Print keywords  . . . . . . . . .
   Help keywords . . . . . . . . . .
   Display sizes . . . . . . . . . .
   Alternate keywords  . . . . . . .


 F3=Exit   F12=Cancel
```

FIGURE 6.43 Choosing indicator keywords

The next screen (Figure 6.44) allows the indicator keyword and indicator choices to be filled in along with a comment that serves only to provide documentation. The screen is shown with the CA03 keyword, the response indicator 99 selection, and the comment filled in.

```
                         Define Indicator Keywords

 Member . . . :    CUSTDSP

Type keywords and parameters, press Enter.
   Conditioned keywords:    CFnn CAnn CLEAR PAGEDOWN/ROLLUP PAGEUP/ROLLDOWN
                            HOME HELP HLPRTN
   Unconditioned keywords:  INDTXT VLDCMDKEY

 Keyword   Indicators/+ Resp Text
 CA03                   99  Exit (End the job)


 F3=Exit   F12=Cancel
```

FIGURE 6.44 CA03 keyword

This finishes the task of defining the screen formats. It would be best to go back to the SELECT screen format and add the text at the bottom of the screen that says, "Press F3 to end the job."

The F3 key is used to back out of the screen design session until the following menu is displayed (Figure 6.45). The default values in the menu are the values you want, so press Enter to create the display file and save the DDS for the screen you designed.

```
                    Save DDS - Create Display File

Type choices, press Enter.

  Save DDS source . . . . . . . . . . . .                    Y=Yes
    Source file . . . . . . . . . . . . .   QDDSSRC          F4 for list
      Library . . . . . . . . . . . . . .   ARLIB            Name, *LIBL ...
    Member . . . . . . . . . . . . . . . .  CUSTDSP          F4 for list
    Text . . . . . . . . . . . . . . . . .  Customer Information Display


  Create display file . . . . . . . . . .                    Y=Yes
    Prompt for parameters . . . . . . . .                    Y=Yes
    Display file . . . . . . . . . . . . .  CUSTDSP          F4 for list
      Library . . . . . . . . . . . . . .   ARLIB            Name, *CURLIB
    Replace existing file . . . . . . . .                    Y=Yes

  Submit create job in batch . . . . . . .                   Y=Yes

  Specify additional save or create options                  Y=Yes

F3=Exit   F4=Prompt   F12=Cancel
```

FIGURE 6.45 Creating display format

Taking the defaults results in two things: A display file object and a source member with the DDS for the object. The next figure (Figure 6.46) uses option 5 from PDM to display the DDS source that SDA generated. Notice its similarity to the DDS used earlier to define physical files. You will also notice a lot of similarity with a few additions.

A DSPSIZ keyword identifies the workstation screen size as 24 lines of display with 80 positions or columns in each line. The CA03 keyword is the one that causes indicator 99 to be turned on when F3 is pressed. On the fourth line you see "4 12'Customer---," etc. Notice that "4" and "12" are the screen coordinates where the constant is located on the screen. The constant that says, "Customer Information Display," is located on line 4 beginning in the twelfth position on that line. Further down the list is the field NAME on the seventh line.

Notice the "I" located a few spaces before the row/line coordinates. The "I" indicates that NAME is an input field on the screen. You will also see two record formats named SELECT and REVIEW. The fields in the REVIEW format have a "B" located where you found the "I" in the NAME field. The "B" indicates that the field (or variable) is used both for output to the screen and as input from the screen to the program. The REFFLD keyword associated with each of the field names is the pointer to the reference file from which SDA retrieved the field attributes.

```
A                                    DSPSIZ(24 80 *DS3)
A                                    CA03(99 'Exit (End the job)')
A     R SELECT
A                                 4 12'Customer Information Display'
A                                 6  4'Select the customer by entering the
A                                      customer''s name'
A                                 9 36'Customer Name'
A       NAME         R        I  9  9REFFLD(REFREC/NAME ARLIB/DICTIONARY)
A     R REVIEW
A                                 5 12'Review the Customer Information'
A       NAME         R        B  9  9REFFLD(REFREC/NAME ARLIB/DICTIONARY)
A                                 9 36'Customer Name'
A       CITY         R        B 11  9REFFLD(REFREC/CITY ARLIB/DICTIONARY)
A       STATE        R        B 11 29REFFLD(REFREC/STATE ARLIB/DICTIONARY)
A                                13 23'Account Balance'
A       BAL          R        B 13  9REFFLD(REFREC/BAL ARLIB/DICTIONARY)
A                                16 10'CREDIT'
A                                17 12'OK?'
A       OK           R        B 18 12REFFLD(REFREC/OK ARLIB/DICTIONARY)
A                                16 32'Date of'
A                                17 30'Last Payment'
A       DTLP         R        B 18 31REFFLD(REFREC/DTLP ARLIB/DICTIONARY)
```

FIGURE 6.46 The DDS source

From this example it is evident that DDS is a source language that describes data for both database files and display files. DDS is also used to describe printed information.

DATA FILE UTILITY

The data file CUSTPF created in the prior section does not yet contain data. A quick way to put data in the file is to use PDM to access the Data File Utility (DFU). To do it, run the STRPDM command to display the menu shown back in Figure 6.14.

Option 2 requests the name of the library from which the objects will be selected. The user keys in the name ARLIB for the library that results in the menu shown in Figure 6.47.

```
                        Work with Objects Using PDM

Library . . . . .    ARLIB              Position to . . . . . . . .
                                        Position to type . . . . .

Type options, press Enter.
  2=Change       3=Copy        4=Delete      5=Display      7=Rename
  8=Display description        9=Save        10=Restore     11=Move ...

Opt  Object       Type     Attribute   Text
__   UPDATE       *PGM     RPG         Review and Update the Customer File
__   CUSTDSP      *FILE    DSPF        Customer Information Display
__   CUSTDSPX     *FILE    DSPF        Customer Information Display
__   CUSTPF       *FILE    PF-DTA      Customer Physical File (
__   DICTIONARY   *FILE    PF-DTA      Data Dictionary (Record name REFREC)
__   QDDSSRC      *FILE    PF-SRC
__   QRPGSRC      *FILE    PF-SRC

Parameters or command
===>____________________________________________________________________
F3=Exit        F4=Prompt            F5=Refresh           F6=Create
F9=Retrieve    F10=Command entry    F23=More options     F24=More keys
```

FIGURE 6.47 Resulting menu

Pressing the F23 key reveals that option 18 selects the DFU. The user wants to add data records to the CUSTPF file, so option 18 is placed alongside the CUSTPF name in the object list as shown in Figure 6.48.

```
                        Work with Objects Using PDM

Library . . . . .   ARLIB              Position to . . . . . . . .
                                       Position to type  . . . . .

Type options, press Enter.
  12=Work with              13=Change text            15=Copy file
  16=Run                    18=Change using DFU       25=Find string ...

Opt  Object        Type     Attribute    Text
___  UPDATE        *PGM     RPG          Review and Update the Customer File
___  CUSTDSP       *FILE    DSPF         Customer Information Display
___  CUSTDSPX      *FILE    DSPF         Customer Information Display
18   CUSTPF        *FILE    PF-DTA       Customer Physical File (
___  DICTIONARY    *FILE    PF-DTA       Data Dictionary (Record name REFREC)
___  QDDSSRC       *FILE    PF-SRC
___  QRPGSRC       *FILE    PF-SRC

Parameters or command
===>_________________________________________________________________
F3=Exit          F4=Prompt              F5=Refresh           F6=Create
F9=Retrieve      F10=Command entry      F23=More options     F24=More keys
```

FIGURE 6.48 Adding data records to the CUSTPF file

The DFU quickly builds a temporary program that allows the user to enter data into the file and make corrections to it. Since the file object contains a description of each field of data, including default column headings for each field, the DFU builds a program that allows records to be entered as shown in Figure 6.49.

```
WORK WITH DATA IN A FILE                                Mode . . . . :   ENTRY
Format . . . . :   CREC                                 File . . . . :   CUSTPF

Customer Name:          ABC CORP
Street Address:         1234 5TH ST
City:                   ANYTOWN
State:                  CA
Zip Code:               97876
Billing Cycle Code:     15
Account Balance:        63899
CREDIT OK?:             Y
Date of Last Payment:   112592


F3=Exit                 F5=Refresh                 F6=Select format
F9=Insert               F10=Entry                  F11=Change
                                   (C) COPYRIGHT IBM CORP. 1980, 1992.
```

FIGURE 6.49 Results of the DFU program

This concludes a very brief look at the DFU. The Data File Utility has many other features that allow the user to identify which specific fields are to be used within the utility, the column headings to be used if the defaults are not wanted, and many other options. The quick sample you saw took the defaults and allowed every field to be changed or added via the utility program that was created by DFU. The complete range of DFU functions can be accessed via the DFU command, STRDFU.

RPG

RPG is a programming language that has enjoyed a great deal of popularity for developing commercial applications. This section shows how to write a simple program that accomplishes the following functions using the two screen formats designed earlier using SDA. The program does the following:

1. Requests the user enter a customer name for an account that is to be reviewed. If the user presses the F3 key, the program ends without checking for a customer name.

2. Retrieves the account information from the account master file and displays the data on the screen. If the customer is not on the file, the program returns to the first step to request another customer name. While the customer information is displayed the user can make changes to any of the displayed data.
3. Updates the customer record when the user has finished making changes (presses the Enter key). If the user presses the F3 key instead of the enter key, the program ends without updating the record.

The logic for this program closely follows the three steps outlined above. The program has a starting point and an ending point with a loop that requests customers records, presents the data, updates the data, and then repeats the cycle until the end of job is signaled. The logic looks like this.

```
START
   While the end of job signal is off (this begins the loop)
      Ask for the next customer by name
      If F3 was pressed, then
         Signal the end of job
         Leave the loop
        Else
           Find the appropriate customer record in the customer file
           If the customer was found in the file, then
              Display the customer information and wait for changes
              If F3 was pressed, then
                 Signal the end of job
                 Leave the loop (ignore any changes entered)
                Else (the changes are OK, F3 was not pressed)
                   Update the customer record in the customer file
              End the if condition
           End the if condition
      End the if condition
   End the while condition (this ends the loop and the loop repeats)
End of the program with end of job signal turned on
```

Before studying the RPG program that follows, you should know several things about the way the code is written.

RPG is a fixed format language. Many programming languages are coded in a free format, but not RPG. RPG programs are columnar; that is, various parts of a line of code (a specification) must be placed in appropriate columns. There is also a strict sequence in which parts of the program must be coded. The simple example that follows uses file specifications and calculation specifications. File specifications must be first and are identified by an "F" in column 6. A "C" in column 6 identifies a calculation specification. A line is treated as a comment if "*" appears in column 7. The RPG program is printed twice for your reference, once with comment lines and again with the comment lines removed.

The following RPG listing has comment lines in it:

```
F*  This line is a comment.  The "*" makes it a comment.
F*  RPG programs use column 6 (The first non-blank column) for
F*  a specification identifier.  This program uses only two
F*  kinds of specification identifiers.
F*  F is the identifier for a file specification.
F*  C is the identifier for a calculation specification.
F*
F*  Two files are defined here.
F*  CUSTPF  (with record format CREC).
F*  This is the database file.
F*  A "UF" follows the file name.  The "U" means it is a
F*  file that is updated, and the "F" means it is a full
F*  function file that is operated on by calculation
F*  specifications.  This program does a CHAIN to get a
F*  record and then does an UPDAT (update) to update the
F*  record.  These operations are performed using the
F*  record name, CREC, not the file name.
F*  The "K" indicates the file is processed randomly
F*  by a key field, in this case NAME is the key field.
F*  Notice the CHAIN operation in calculation specifications.
F*
F*  CUSTDSP is a display file with two formats, SELECT and REVIEW.
F*  The following file name indicates that combined
F*  output/input operations are valid using this display
F*  file.  The "F" indicates that it is a full function file
F*  and the EXFMT (execute format) operation is used in
F*  calculation specifications to output a format, then read
F*  for input when the Enter key is pressed or F3 is pressed.
F*
F*  Both file specifications have an E coded in the line.
F*  The E identifies these files as external objects,
F*  and consequently the program extracts all fields from
F*  these file objects. This defines the field names
F*  as variables with all the correct attributes known
F*  to the program. No other definition of these
F*  variables is necessary or allowed.
F*
FCUSTPF  UF  E           K        DISK
FCUSTDSP CF  E                    WORKSTN
F*
C*  File specifications have ended: Calculation specifications begin
C*  When the "C" is followed by "*," it is a comment line.
C*
C*  In RPG when LR is on, the job is signaled to end.
C*  RPG uses indicators to signal various conditions.
C*  The last record indicator, LR, is checked in a DO WHILE
C*  loop where *INLR is the indicator name and
C*  DOWEQ means DO WHILE EQUAL, i.e. loop while LR is off.
C*
C*  In RPG calculations, an operator operates on factor 1
C*  and factor 2.  Some operations turn on indicators.
```

```
C*  Indicators are turned on in columns just to the left
C*  of the comment field.  Two indicators, LR and 77, are
C*  turned on by a SETON operation and a CHAIN operation.
C*
C*       Factor1    Oper Factor 2                          Comments
C        *INLR      DOWEQ*OFF                              START LOOP
C*  The EXFMT operation displays the SELECT format.
C                   EXFMTSELECT                            ASK (SELECT)
C*  IFEQ means if equal -- if indicator 99 is on.
C        *IN99      IFEQ *ON                               F3 PRESSED?
C*  The SETON operation turns on indicator LR -- last record.
C                   SETON                            LR    END JOB
C                   LEAVE                                  LEAVE LOOP
C                   ELSE
C*  The name of the customer we want to update was provided
C*  as a result of the previous EXFMT SELECT operation.
C*  Indicator 77 is turned on if the customer is not found.
C        NAME       CHAINCREC                        77    FIND RECORD D
C        *IN77      IFEQ *OFF                              IF FOUND
C*  Display the REVIEW format and allow fields to be updated.
C*  The EXFMT operation ends when either Enter or F3 is pressed.
C                   EXFMTREVIEW                            REVIEW
C        *IN99      IFEQ *ON                               F3 PRESSED?
C                   SETON                            LR    END JOB
C                   LEAVE                                  LEAVE LOOP
C                   ELSE
C*  Update the customer record
C*  Data in the REVIEW format that was changed also appears in the
C*  record named CREC so that the data is updated in the following
C*  UPDAT operation that updates CREC.  All of the changes take
C*  place without the program needing to reference the field names.
C*  Nothing prevents the program from such references, but none are
C*  needed in this program.
C                   UPDATCREC                              UPDATE
C                   ENDIF
C                   ENDIF
C                   ENDIF
C                   ENDDO                                  END LOOP
C*  This is the end of the program.  If the LR indicator is on,
C*  the program ends.
```

The RPG program is listed again below with all comment lines removed. The short comments on the right side of the calculation specifications remain.

```
FCUSTPF  UF  E           K        DISK
FCUSTDSP CF  E                    WORKSTN
C           *INLR     DOWEQ*OFF                       START LOOP
C                     EXFMTSELECT                     ASK (SELECT)
C           *IN99     IFEQ *ON                        F3 PRESSED?
C                     SETON                     LR    END JOB
C                     LEAVE                           LEAVE LOOP
C                     ELSE
```

```
C           NAME      CHAINCREC                 77  FIND RECORD D
C           *IN77     IFEQ *OFF                     IF FOUND
C                     EXFMTREVIEW                   REVIEW
C           *IN99     IFEQ *ON                      F3 PRESSED?
C                     SETON                     LR  END JOB
C                     LEAVE                         LEAVE LOOP
C                     ELSE
C                     UPDATCREC                     UPDATE
C                     ENDIF
C                     ENDIF
C                     ENDIF
C                     ENDDO                         END LOOP
```

Perhaps it seems odd that the only variable name referenced in this program is NAME. The reason is that all of the variables are field names in the records, and the program deals with them on a record basis by naming the formats CREC in the database file and formats SELECT and REVIEW in the display file. If the program needed to make reference to fields such as BAL, DTLP, etc., the program could do so without needing to define them first. Thus the CHAIN operation finds the record with the customer name found in NAME. The record is named CREC. When the record is presented to the program, all of the fields, NAME, ADDR, CITY, STATE, ZIP, etc., are available to the program. Figure 6.50 shows how this program works.

The program is named UPDATE, and it is executed by calling it with the following CALL command:

```
CALL UPDATE
```

The program begins running at the top of the calculation specifications. The first visual evidence the user sees is in the result of the EXFMT operation that presents the SELECT screen. Assuming that the user keyed in the name XYZ CORP as the name of the customer to be selected for review, the screen would appear as shown in Figure 6.50 after keying in the customer name.

```
        Customer Information Display

Select the customer by entering the customer's name


    XYZ CORP_________________    Customer Name
```

FIGURE 6.50 Selecting customer name

After the company name, XYZ CORP, is keyed into the input field, the Enter key is pressed, and the program continues to execute. You will recall from the way the SELECT format was designed that the name of the variable into which the company name was typed is NAME. The variable field NAME now contains the data XYZ CORP. The program uses the NAME field to find the record for the XYZ CORP via the CHAIN operation. In RPG, the CHAIN operation results in retrieving the record with NAME, ADDR, CITY, STATE, etc. from the file. The following EXFMT in Figure 6.51 displays the REVIEW format.

```
      Review the Customer Information

  XYZ CORP__________________  Customer Name

  ROCHESTER           MN

    $639.00     Account Balance

   CREDIT                  Date of
     OK?                Last Payment
     Y                     8/05/92
```

FIGURE 6.51 REVIEW format after an EXFMT operation

Some of these fields are named in the REVIEW format; consequently, they are displayed. You will recall from the discussion about defining the REVIEW format that all of these fields were defined as both output and input fields. Consequently, the data in the fields is displayed and the user is able to change any of that data. Upon making any changes and pressing the Enter key, the program regains control and rewrites the record with all changed fields via the UPDAT operation, which updates the record with the CREC format name. The original record contained the name ANYTOWN in the CITY field, and the operator has changed it to ROCHESTER. Consequently, the CITY value is changed in this record in the database.

This rather simple program reveals some important facts about the AS/400 that should be noted by persons who approach this system from a PC background.

The first is that the object-oriented approach shown in this chapter points to the simplicity of writing programs that manage database information. This is particularly true when data must be presented interactively on a workstation screen where it is viewed and/or acted upon. With proper screen design, the programmer is relieved from the tiresome duty of mapping the data on the screen and writing routines that collect related data together before acting upon them as a whole collection of related data. The screen format does that for the programmer.

A second fact of importance is that in order to reap the maximum benefits of these productivity factors, the database definition must be given careful attention upfront. The application designer should know as much as possible about what data will be needed, maximum lengths and values, how data will be presented on reports and display screens, and how data should be organized in the database.

When these concepts are grasped and exploited by application developers, the task of implementing applications is greatly enhanced. This accounts for the high ratings given to the system for application productivity. Many application development efforts in a commercial environment, however, spend up to 80 percent of their resources maintaining existing code. This is where the AS/400 is especially productive. Very often the changes that must be made are changes to the database. As new data fields are added, field sizes changed, or other changes take place, they are reflected first in the reference file (like the file named DICTIONARY) and then in the physical files and logical files that make up the database. Using this object-oriented approach means that a relatively simple process can be followed to recreate the files and then the programs that use them. Changes in field sizes and definitions are brought forward into the new files and new programs. Programs need to be changed only when they use new fields or when the usage of existing data changes in some way. Most of the tedious and error-prone tasks of updating programs or data are eliminated.

One must remember to save the data from physical files before they are changed so that the saved data can be copied to the files with the new definitions. A few programmers new to the AS/400 have discovered to their dismay that they recreated a physical file and took the option to delete the file so that a new one could be created, but forgot to save the data first. The system has a Copy File Utility (CPYF) that makes the task easy and does what would require a separate program on most systems.

While editing of the RPG program was not shown here, it is worth noting that the Source Entry Utility, SEU, is used to edit RPG source programs just as SEU was used to edit the DDS for physical files. SEU recognizes the correct formats for RPG specifications and supports both prompting and syntax checking for RPG source just as it did for DDS source. Thus the programmer is freed from having to know which source column is used for which function when programming in RPG.

SUMMARY

This chapter described and illustrated the process for creating objects from source definitions. The process is consistent and requires the editing of a source member that defines the object, then uses the compile option (or create command) to create the object from the source definition. These steps apply to a reference file that serves as a data dictionary, a physical file, a display file, and an RPG program. In the examples in this chapter four objects were created: A reference file, a physical file, a display file, and a program. The program used a display file to allow the user to request the name of a customer whose account was to be reviewed. The program used the program name to look for that customer in the physical file and then used another format in the display file to display the data. The data were displayed as fields that allowed changes to the displayed data. The user treated all input data on the screen as a complete form. The concept is much like filling out a paper form with a lead pencil and an eraser, which allows changes before committing the entire form. The program then took the changed data and updated the appropriate record in the physical file so that the changes made on the display screen were reflected in the database file.

The key to making this kind of activity simple is to exploit the object-oriented architecture of the AS/400. The place to start in a commercial application is with a reference file that serves as the data dictionary for all data in physical files and display files.

7

High-Level Languages

What is the best way to design a total computer system? Divide up the task between several independent groups and have them develop their own standards and implement various pieces to be integrated later? Probably not, but there is a long tradition for that technique, not promoted by design, but by history. Someone develops a basic machine, then others come along and "flesh it out." They add their own creativity to the pool. The result is little consistancy in operation, lots of incompatibility, and data usable only by selected applications.

The S/38 developers had a new opportunity. With the worldwide popularity of the earlier S/3, S/32, and S/34 machines, they knew their audience and its needs. Most of the potential customers programmed in RPG, but not exclusively. There were many COBOL users as well. In general, people wanted a commercial machine to manage businesses with a lot of data.

So what should a complete system have? Utilities? Languages? A database? Yes, but many computers had those. What made the S/38 different was that these components were designed together. Using an integrated database as the only way to store data meant absolute consistency in accessing data. Utilities had been unorganized collections of dissimilar programs, but the S/38 combined them in an expandable control language. Since CL is a language, it was given power one normally expects only in high-level languages—it could be interpreted or compiled. Compiled CL programs could be run as traditional programming languages, so the natural choice was to make all language interfaces compatible. Any language could call any language on the S/38. Any language could be used for the main program.

Databases were becoming very popular and were great places to store data definitions. The S/38 incorporated database concepts into not only its data file management system, but all files; printer files, disk files, and workstation files were all consistent. For users who chose to use external data definitions—definitions in data files—there was a single data language, DDS (Data Description Specifications), and any language could use those definitions.

S/38 grew up to become the AS/400, and the theme of consistency guided that growth. Its consistent file and programming language interfaces let programmers use their favorite language, knowing that they were benefiting from most of the AS/400's strengths. Multilingual programmers also had the freedom to choose the best language for a given job.

MIXING AS/400 LANGUAGES

Since any AS/400 language can create both main programs and subprograms, you can pick the best language to handle any part of a given task. You can write a collection of subprograms to perform your standard tasks and then select any of them for the function it performs without regard to its source language. Top-down, bottom-up, structured—whatever your programming style, this modularity simplifies your work and adds efficiency.

RPG III/400

While most languages have a programming background, RPG does not. It was based upon the old line of IBM unit record equipment. The old cardboard punched card was the "unit record." People who understood the machines, which read data from the cards, punched holes in them, printed their contents, and arranged their sequences, were the intended audience. They understood that you could plug one end of a wire into a "hub" (a socket in a patch panel) to get data from card column 1, and the other end of the wire into another hub to carry the data to print position 1. If the field was seven digits wide, seven wires were used.

The patch panel had an input section with 80 hubs for the 80 columns of data in the cards and 47 hubs in the alphanumeric output section—just enough to print "The International Business Machines Corporation."

Programming with Wires

The phrase "words for wires" sold the concept. No longer would you have to grab a fistful of wires to carry data from the input section to the output section. With RPG, you could just write a word, any word, on the input page and the same word on the output page. That word was "the bunch of wires" carrying the data.

Programming with Words

"Page" in this case was a simple concept; a piece of paper with "I" preprinted in position 6 on each line if it was an input sheet. It was divided into columns where specifications had to be placed. The word, or field name, had to be in positions 53 through 58. Names began with an alphabetic character. The rest of the up to six character names could be either alphabetic or numeric. The only special characters permitted were "&," "$," and "#." These rules led to some creative, while concise, names such as AMT rather than END_OF_MONTH_BALANCE.

The way that the source code was made machine-readable was to put it in punched cards with a keypunch machine, sort of a typewriter that poked holes in cardboard. Since those keypunches were monocase, RPG is, too. Except for quoted constants, all source is in uppercase.

ELEMENTS OF RPG

The humble name, Report Program Generator, indicated the modest expectations for the language. It is barely more than specifications for a utility program used to generate reports, but it has some rather powerful, specialized functions. For instance, reports often list a number of records for one customer followed by some totals, blank lines, then the records for another customer.

That common task requires a programmer to define a hold field. The program then moves the customer number into the hold field for the first record of a group and compares the following records with it. When a different value is read, the new data is held back back so they do not mix in with the previous group, and the program signals that a control break has occurred so that total calculations and printing can be done.

An RPG programmer accomplishes all of that by writing "L1" in positions 59 and 60 beside the customer-number field name on the input sheet. Simple.

The "L" is for "level," and "1" is the lowest of up to nine levels. L1 lets reports group items within "item" class, within "warehouse," within "customer," within "salesman," within "area," within "region," within. . .well, you get the idea. L1 is not only a flag to identify a control field, it is an "indicator," a 1 byte field that contains either a "1" or "0" representing on or off, respectively. It is used to handle total calculations and output. It also stays on through the processing of the first record of the new group, so it can also handle special printing and output associated with the start of a new group. . .like skipping to a new page and printing a heading. RPG turns L1 on and off for you. To be consistent, RPG even turns L1 on for the very first record the program reads, on the assumption that it is the first record of the first group.

As you may have guessed, the output page has an "O" in position 6. Because of differing requirements for output, the name goes in different locations than input, which uses positions 32 through 37. This may seem confusing, but the AS/400 editor SEU (Source Entry Utility) understands these differences and will prompt you.

There is a calculations page, too. It has a "C" in position 6, and columns set aside for factor 1, an operation code, factor 2, and a result. An RPG calculation might look like:

```
CL1    QTY    MULT    UPRICE    AMOUNT 72
```

L1, which is immediately after the C, makes this a total calculation to be performed after the last record of the group. It multiplies QTY by UPRICE and puts the product in a field called AMOUNT. AMOUNT is defined here as having seven digits of which two are to the right of the decimal point.

Here is an interesting contrast:

```
C   L1                         MOVE INT         NEWINT 2
```

This time the L1 does not come right after the C. The blanks in positions 7 and 8 make this a detail calculation. L1 remains on through the processing of a group's first record, so this calculation moves INT from the first record of a group to a field named NEWINT. NEWINT is defined here as a two character field. The blank in the decimal positions field makes this a character field. The other fields, QTY, UPRICE, and INT, are defined somewhere else—on input, another calculation, or even outside of the program in a data file of some sort. Remember that AS/400 files not only contain data, but also the definitions of the data they hold. Simply referring to a file makes its definitions available to RPG.

Files are identified on the (yes, yet another page) file description page. It has an "F" in position 6. Starting in position 7 you enter the name of the file you want and an "E" in position 19, which means "externally described." RPG will go find the file and fill in the field names and their definitions. This saves you the problems of creating correct definitions. If the file's definitions are ever changed, your program will not run, which protects you from damaging the data with out-of-date programs. The fix may be as simple as recompiling your old, unchanged source. RPG will pick up the new definitions, and your program will be able to run again.

Compiling and Running

Some languages interpret source code during execution, but RPG does not. Instead you have to compile the source code before you can run the program. Your source is kept in a member of a source file.

```
CRTRPGPGM  PGM(MYPROG)  SRCFILE(QRPGSRC)
```

The CL command above runs the RPG compiler and tells it to create a program called MYPROG, to look for the source in a file called QRPGSRC, and to assume that the member name is MYPROG, the same as the program name. The compiler will look for all of the external files the specs reference, include their data definitions, and pick up a “check” number from each of the files. If you have no serious errors, you will end up with a program. To run the program, just enter:

```
CALL   MYPROG
```

Your program will find all the files it references and compare the check number it got during compilation with the current check number in each file. If they all agree, the program will read, calculate, and write according to your specifications. The check number is what keeps old programs from running with changed files. Significant alterations change the number.

Most programmers use the Programming Development Manager, PDM, so programming and testing is simplified. Select SEU for entry. After entering the specs, you put the compile option number beside your program’s name. After compilation, you put the call option beside your program’s name. It is as simple as that.

By the way, the RPG compiler prints, but otherwise ignores statements with a valid character in position 6 and an asterisk in 7. That is how you enter comments into your programs.

File Description Specifications

You just read about referencing externally described files. RPG lets you define files internally, too. These are called "program-described" files. Just put a different character in position 19, an "F" for fixed length records. You have the responsibility of supplying that record length. Yes, there is a place for it.

For either a program or externally described file, you have to tell RPG how you are going to read or write it, what kind of device it is, and whether it is to be read or written. If it is a disk file to be written, will you be adding records to the end of existing records or starting with record 1? If the file is to be read, are you going to read the whole thing from the beginning? Are you going to read the records in their physical sequence, in the sequence of an index, or in a random sequence? If random, will you be using an index or a relative record number to find the records? Are you going to be updating the records? If it is a printer, who is going to handle page overflow, you or RPG?

There are codes for each of these decisions. "I" is for input. "O" is for output. "U" is for update. "A" is for add. "K" is for key, which is the way to reach a record through an index. "OF" is for printer page overflow.

Like L1, OF is an indicator. It comes on whenever the printer comes to the end of a page. You will usually use it to skip to a new page and print a heading, but if you ignore it, you will print right over the perforations in the paper. If you leave it out entirely, RPG will automatically skip to a new page for you.

File Extension Specifications

This page has an "E" in column 6, and it is used for defining arrays. Arrays violate good database design, so there is no way to define them externally. RPG III, however, does give you a way to equate arrays to external data.

Arrays may be referenced by entirety or by element. Using just the name of an array, such as "ARRY," RPG knows you mean the entire array. Following the name with a subscript tells RPG you want only one element: "ARRY,X." In this case "X" must be a numeric field with no decimal places. Use short names, because the whole reference including the comma may need to fit in a 6-position space on a coding form.

RPG III does all of its arithmetic in decimal. Addressing, on the other hand, is in binary. As a result, a subscript you develop has to be converted to binary before it can be used. That is a time-consuming process on any machine.

Feel free to use subscripts in RPG III, but don't overuse them. If you are, for instance, planning to parse very long character streams, RPG III may not be the language for that job.

RPG III does have a powerful table lookup instruction, LOKUP, which often makes subscripts unnecessary. Also, hard-coded subscripts, such as ARRY,10, are resolved by the compiler and require no extra processing when you run your program.

Input Specifications

You've read about the L1 and OF indicators. RPG has several more specialized indicators that it sets on and off, but the 99 general indicators, "01," "02," . . . , "99," are used the most. On the input page, you can assign them to specialized functions. For instance, to the right of a field name are three places for indicators to check for positive, negative, and zero values in each field. Just put the indicator of your choice in the negative position, and the indicator will be set with each read—on for negative and off for zero or positive. For character fields, the zero position checks for all blanks. An indicator used this way is called a field indicator.

Above the field specification lines is a specification for the record. Since RPG was designed to work with 80-character records, it was often impossible to get all of the data in just one record. To keep multicard records straight, a record code was included (an "A" in column 1 of the first record, a "B" in the second, and so forth). There is a place to specify up to 3 code tests on a record specification line as well as a place to put a general indicator. RPG sets the record identifying indicator on and off for you. Even though AS/400 applications rarely use record codes, record identifying indicators are still handy.

```
imaster       01
idetail       02
i                                            amt         33
```

The input specifications for an externally described logical database file listed above identify the record types by their database-supplied names. Whenever a master record is read, indicator 01 will be on, and 02 will be on for detail records.

Externally described files automatically make all of their fields available to the program, so no field specifications are required. However in this case, I wanted to know when AMT was negative, so I included a line for it with a field indicator, 33, in the (trust me) minus position.

Program-described input files are rare. They discard many of the AS/400 database advantages by requiring you to specify every field you need along with its location and definition.

Calculation Specifications

RPG has a built-in flowchart, and the calculation specifications are part of it. The following is typical processing logic:

```
input
calculations
output
```

In the early life of RPG, its flowchart was rigidly followed; there was no other option. Now, however, new calculation operations let you do everything from the calculations page. You can control the logic.

Indicators can condition calculation lines. Each line has space for 3 indicator tests, joined by "and"s. If that isn't enough, you can have more lines by using both "and" and "or" logic. The following is an example of Boolean logic conditioning a calculation:

```
c      02 15
c or   02n33                 updatdetail
```

Whenever RPG comes to the statement above, the DETAIL record is updated if indicator 02 is on, and either 15 is on or 33 is off.

RPG normally tries to execute all calculations in sequence, leaving it to your indicators to prevent instructions from operating if they are not needed at that time. Internally, RPG tests the indicators, and if the test fails, it jumps over the instruction. Unconditioned calculations generally operated too often, so they used to be rare.

Indicators were the life blood of RPG, but that is changing. With *if-else*, *do*, *do while*, *do until*, *case*, *subroutines*, and *go to*, you can direct RPG to just the statements you want executed. So unconditioned calculations are common now.

```
c            baldue    ifgt crlim
c                      exsr over
c                      end
```

In this example of indicator-free calculations, BALDUE is compared to CRLIM. If BALDUE is greater, the program executes a subroutine called OVER. You will notice there are no indicators in sight.

Printing Reports

Even though output is often generated now from calculations, output specifications are frequently used to describe what is to be written. This is particularly true for program-described files. Printer files may be externally described, but often are not, so you'll see lots of printing details in RPG programs.

```
oqprint  h  2 1   1p
o        or       of
o                                  60 'customer report'
o                         page  z  80
```

This is an internally described printing, which is the typical way to program a report so that a title will be printed at the top of each page. It uses the standard AS/400 print file, QPRINT. The "H" means this is a heading. The printer will skip to line 1 before printing and then use double-spacing afterward. There are space-before, space-after, skip-before, and skip-after positions. This heading is conditioned by two indicators: OF, the overflow indicator we discussed, and "1P." RPG sets 1P on at the beginning so that the first-page heading can be printed, then RPG turns it off. You can turn it on again if you want, but RPG will not.

Following these two record specification lines are the field specifications. CUSTOMER REPORT will print ending in position 60 at the top of the page, and a page number will print ending in position 80. PAGE is one of eight automatic counters in RPG. It starts at 1, and every time you use it, it increments by 1. Leading zeros will be suppressed by the "Z."

Since RPG was created to print reports, its built-in flowchart is usually the logic you need. RPG's real flow is more like this:

```
heading and detail output
total calculations
total output
input
detail calculations
```

The first thing a report needs is a heading, so the first thing RPG tries to do is print it. Since you are just starting, there are no total calculations or output performed, but the ninth level indicators will be on to start processing the first record.

After giving you the data from the new record, RPG drops into the calculation page and tries to perform all of the calculations with blanks in columns 7 and 8. These are the detail calculations.

When the program moves out of the bottom of the detail calculations, it returns to print the heading and detail output again. This time, however, the 1P indicator is off, but there will be a record identifying the on indicator, which you probably used to condition output. Below are record-identifying indicators used on output specifications:

```
o       d      01
o                       cus#        8
o                       cname      25
o       d      02
o                       item       20
o                       amt    j   40
```

After getting a master record, the above block of RPG coding will print CUS# and CNAME, then skip over the rest of the output. On the next cycle with the detail record, it will print ITEM and AMT on a new line (it defaults to single spacing). "D" stands for detail and "J" is an edit code. It suppresses leading zeros from the AMT field, inserts commas and a decimal point, and supplies a minus sign on the right for negative values.

Total Processing

The preceding example does not lend itself to total processing because every group begins with a master record. Checking for a level break to find the beginning of a group would be redundant.

The following example illustrates typical report-writing techniques. To make the program especially easy, we will use externally described database and printer files.

```
fitems    ip  e           k       disk
finvlist  o   e             of    printer
I*
iirec         01
i                                             class 12
i                                             itm#  11
I*
c   01                 add  qty       tot
```

```
cl1                   add  tot       ctot
cl2                   add  ctot      ftot
O*
oheading  h       12
o       or        of
o                     *all
oitmline  d       01
o                     *all
oItmtot   t       l1
o                     tot    b
oclasstot t       l2
o                     ctot   b
ofintot   t       lr
o                     *all
```

This is a fairly involved RPG report that prints a detail line for each input record. It processes several records for each item and accumulates totals for each item, class of items, and for the whole inventory. Between the database and printer files, all of the fields are defined externally. You really cannot tell how much detail is listed since the printer will get all of the fields it wants, and the database will supply all of the fields needed.

ITEMS, the database file, is input primary, "IP." Primary means that the file will be read automatically from beginning to end, and then RPG will turn on the "LR," the last record indicator. If LR is on after total output, the program quits. Fortunately, that is just what we want.

The sequence of specifications is quite natural, leading from the details to larger and larger totals. However, this is not the sequence in which they will be executed. The RPG compiler will move the total calculations and output to the corresponding parts of its flowchart. Within each type, however, the sequence will be maintained.

The first calculation accumulates each record's QTY into a field called TOT. You will notice that the program did not have to initialize that field. RPG starts with zeros in all numeric fields and blanks in all character fields.

The second calculation rolls TOT into ITOT. Of course, TOT must be cleared for the next group. That is what the "B" on output does. It blanks (zeros) TOT after sending its contents to the printer.

In this example, only the fields needing resetting after printing appear on output, otherwise "*ALL" would have done the trick. *ALL sends all of the fields the printer wants, and so it requires less thought.

The indicators you may not have figured out are in the heading. "L2" prints a heading at the beginning. RPG begins with all "L-" indicators on. Then every time the class of items changes, L2 comes on. So the report will have each class begin on a new page. If the items of a class fill a page, OF will head up the additional pages. The descriptive names starting in position 7 (HEADING, ITMLINE, ITMTOT, etc.) are the record names used in the printer file's external description. Skipping, spacing, constants, and field locations are all described in detail there. This example clearly demonstrates one of the advantages of externally described files. The clutter of definition details are somewhere else, so the program logic is clear.

DATABASE PROCESSING

Database files can be processed on RPG input and output specifications, but specialized operations make the calculation page the best place to do it for most programs. READ gives you the next record in the file. CHAIN reads any record you specify. After you have read a record, UPDAT writes it back along with any changes you may have made to its data. While WRITE adds a new record to the database, DELET takes one away.

```
fpartmastuf  e                          disk
ftfile    if  e        k                disk
C            *IN99     DOuEQ'1'
c                     read master                   99
c   n99      itm      chaintrans
c   n99               updatmaster
c                     end
c                     seton                         lr
```

The master file update calculations above illustrate the power of external descriptions and RPG's operations. It reads the PARTMAST file from beginning to end. If PARTMAST is a physical file, which has only one record format, the program could have read from either the file name or the record name, because they would work exactly the same. On the other hand, the results will be different if reading from a logical file with several record names. Reading from the file name gives you the next record along the access path without regard to its name. Reading from the record name skips over any intervening records with other names.

In the master file update calculations above, when RPG tries to read beyond the end of the MASTER file, indicator 99 will come on, and the program will skip the following operations and terminate the "do until" loop. SETON at the end turns on the LR indicator. When we come to the bottom of calculations, RPG will have a chance to detect that LR is on and end the program.

The "do until" command, DOU, is compressed to fit the old RPG format. DOU followed by the comparison type, just fits in the five spaces for operation code. EQ says that when *IN99 is equal to the character 1, the loop will end. *IN99 is a reference to indicator 99, as if *IN99 were just a one character data field.

You will notice that the only database datum mentioned is ITM, the item number. ITM contains the key data to the transaction file. The "K" in the middle of the TFILE file description tells RPG to use TFILE's index to find its records. Summarizing, READ picks up a master file record containing lots of fields. . .including ITM. CHAIN reads the TFILE record (yes, I can use TFILE instead of the record name, TRANS) containing new data for that item. Since the external descriptions of both files use the same field names, CHAIN automatically replaces the old values from the master file. UPDAT rewrites the master file record with new data.

Looking at the file description specifications above, you can see that the master file is to be updated. It has a "U" in position 15. The transaction file, marked with an "I," is for input only. The "F" in position 16 of both files means "fully procedural," which prompts the program to do its input/output (I/O) with calculation specifications.

Look at the PARTMAST file description. There is no K, so there is no index. It will be read in the physical sequence of its records. This is generally the sequence in which they were originally written, and it may differ from the sequence of its index. I could have specified a K. The results would have been the same, but the program may have taken longer because the AS/400 would have had to read the index and select the records in a random sequence. AS/400 indexes are very fast, but not using one is even faster. Processing in physical sequence, the AS/400 will read a block of several records with each access, and it will also double buffer so it can read the next block while the current one is being processed. Both of these techniques are applied automatically and will speed up the program.

If you took a critical look at my logic, you would have noticed that the program expects a transaction record for each master record. Unrealistic? Maybe not. If missing transactions are normal, how can they be handled? That could be the normal situation. Here is part of the last example, but modified to allow for a few missing transactions:

```
c  n99   itm       chaintrans          50
c  n50
corn99             updatmaster
```

When CHAIN fails to find a record, it will turn on the indicator specified in the position where you see indicator 50. Not indicator 50 is ored to the update line. If 50 is on, there was no transaction record for this item, so the UPDAT is skipped.

Keeping in mind AS/400 record blocking, is it really important to skip the UPDAT? When the AS/400 finishes processing a block of records, it will write the whole block whether or not all of the records were updated, and updating with no new data puts the original data back. So the results will be the same whether or not the UPDAT is skipped, and the difference in speed would be negligible.

Suppose that instead of a few missing transaction records, there were many. Maybe there are a million records in the master file and only a hundred in the transaction file. The program above would work fine, but much too hard. It would process 1,000,100 records. Changing the program logic, that could be lowered to just 200 records processed—100 transactions and the 100 corresponding master records.

```
fpartmastuf  e        K            disk
ftfile     if  e                   disk
C          *IN99       DOuEQ"1"
c                     read trans              99
c                     move qty     qsave  70
c     n99  itm        chainmaster
c                     move qsave   qty
c     n99             updatmaster
c                     end
c                     seton                        lr
```

Here the logic is reversed. The program reads through the transaction file and chains to the master file. The major changes are the file that has the K and switching the files referenced by the READ and CHAIN.

A new problem does pop up. Since both files use the same field names, reading the master file after the transaction file would replace the new transaction data with old master data. To avoid that, the program saves the fields to be changed (in this simple case, only QTY) and moves them back after the CHAIN.

WORKSTATION PROCESSING

To make a program interactive, you use a workstation file. That allows the program to communicate directly with its user. You saw that database files are declared to be input, output, or update. Most workstation files are combined, for which a "C" is put in position 16 of the file description.

While you can WRITE and READ a workstation file, you will generally use the combined WRITE/READ operation, EXFMT (execute format), since that is the typical way to interact with users. You WRITE a workstation format to the screen, then READ it. The READ waits for the operator to enter data. Occasionally you may have a lot of work to do in a program and can hide some of the processing time by using separate WRITE and READ statements. Just WRITE the format, finish up processing, then READ the format. The AS/400 handles the workstation input while your program processes. If it READs before the operator finishes keying, the operator will not know the program was paying no attention to him or her.

The AS/400 always handles an operator's keystrokes whether you use WRITE/READ or EXFMT. So the AS/400 will prevent you from writing programs that analyze each keystroke as do word processors with dynamic wordwrap. Keystrokes are handled by separate processors not directly available to you.

Here is an example of simple inquiry. The workstation file is an externally defined display file and contains only one format. To keep from confusing the operator, the results portion of the screen will be blank initially. In response to the first request we will display the same format, but this time the results will appear and the input field will be blank, ready for the next inquiry. Fortunately, most of this work is handled by the external file definition and controlled by passing indicators between the program and file.

```
fuser      cf  e                      workstn
ffile      if  e          k           disk
c           *IN99     doueq"1"
c                     exfmtscreen
c    n99    itmnbr    chainrecord
c                     seton           25LR
c                     end
```

SCREEN, the workstation file's format, has the result portion of the screen conditioned by indicator 25 in the above example. Since RPG begins with all general indicators off, the first EXFMT will display only the request for an inquiry and the input only field ITMNBR. Of course, the operator does not see that name, only a well-designed screen with a friendly prompt. Also, SCREEN defines function key 3, which turns on indicator 99 when it is pressed. The reason you do not see most of these details is that they are in the external display file.

When the operator enters the item number of interest and presses Enter, the program regains control and CHAINs to the database file, then sets indicators 25 and LR on. Indicator 25 will be used on the subsequent trips through the DO loop to display the inquiry results.

Setting LR on might seem premature, but it makes no difference in this situation. RPG doesn't get a chance to detect that LR is on until we drop out of the loop.

When the operator is finished, he or she presses function key 3. That returns control to the program with indicator 99 on, which will terminate the loop and let RPG terminate the program. You might think that using LR in the external display file definition instead of 99 would be a good idea. However, only numeric indicators (01 through 99) can be passed between programs and files.

COMMUNICATIONS PROGRAMMING

On the AS/400, the primary difference between workstation and communications programming is that errors are likely to happen in communications. ICF (the Intersystem Communication Function) makes communications files similar to workstation files, complete with externally described data, formats, and indicators. In fact, a simple communications program could function as well as a normal interactive program.

All files in your programs have I/O feedback areas you can reach with RPG. Normally, you do not need that information, but for communications, you may. For instance, suppose a storm had just destroyed the communication link, so you would not want to burn up valuable machine time retrying the operation. On the other hand, other problems tend to be of short duration and trying again may be all that it takes. In other situations, you might have to close and reopen the file. The major/minor return codes in the I/O feedback area tell you the problem and what, if anything, might correct it. The ICF manual documents the codes and recommended actions.

C LANGUAGE FOR THE AS/400

The AS/400 was developed with no user access to an assembler language, which is not so bad because there are very few tasks users cannot perform with high-level languages such as RPG III and COBOL. But there are existing applications written in languages with assembler-like capabilities, and there is an occasional need to get closer to the system than high level languages permit. That is why C/400, a flavor of C for the AS/400, was developed.

The C language in general does not fit the expectations of the AS/400, so the AS/400 builds a special "environment" whenever a main C/400 program initiates. This environment contains your global definitions, the stack, and heap, and subsequent C programs can run in the same environment and share global definitions. Creating an environment is a significant task for the system. You should try to limit the number of creations as much as possible. If you have a C routine you would like to call to perform a small function for an RPG or COBOL program, you should consider rewriting it in RPG or COBOL. The creation of a new environment may not be offset by whatever time savings (if any) you can achieve by using C.

In high-level languages, subprograms generally perform significant amounts of work. Even though AS/400 calls use quite a few instructions, the call processing time tends to be negligible with respect to the amount of work the subroutine performs. That, however is not true of many C routines, which often perform very small tasks. Calling such a routine, even without causing an environment to be created, is a significant investment in call processing. Such routines should be replaced with in-line code or macros.

AS/400 hardware is optimized to perform commercial tasks. Many operations that people write in C have scientific or numeric characteristics. As a result, the AS/400 may not be able to keep up with a smaller processor with better stack-handling instructions and other scientific or numeric abilities. That all sounds very negative. It is, however, designed to help you choose wisely how to best use the C/400 language.

THE C/400 LANGUAGE

C/400 follows ANSI standards and meets SAA Level 2 standard as well. It has IBM extensions for conversion of commercial data, access to database, commitment control, Structured Query Language, I/O feedback from files, interlanguage calls, GDDM (for graphics), and double-byte character sets. Double-byte character sets are for alphabets with more than 256 characters in them.

C/400 programs run in an Extended Program Model (EPM). The EPM includes the environment, extensions to the AS/400 debugger to access C programs and data, support for exception handlers, multiple-entry-point programs, and a session handler. The most important part of that is that when EPM is needed, the AS/400 will provide it; and with it, C can do what it should.

More specifically, the AS/400 does not really understand the scope of variables in C. EPM does. AS/400 does not understand including ".h" files. EPM does. C uses lots of standard functions AS/400 does not have. EPM includes them.

Compiling and Running a C/400 program

You put your source code into a member of a source file for a program on the AS/400. The Source Entry Utility (SEU) editor can be used for direct entry, or you could copy an existing file from a PC. If you enter your program on a dumb terminal, you may find you are missing some keys you need for C. SEU recognizes some trigraphs that fill in those gaps. For instance, "??(" and "??)" represent left and right square brackets, respectively.

```
CRTCPGM    MYPROG
```

When your source program is in, use the CRTCPGM command to initiate the compiler, as in the above example. The compiler assumes the source program is in a member of the source file QCSRC, and the name of the member is the same as the name of your program. CRTCPGM has an optional DEFINE parameter that lets you insert source definitions that act as if they were part of your source file. DEFINE is generally added for conditional compiles.

```
CALL MYPROG
```

After compilation, use the CALL command to run your program, as in the above example. Using the Program Development Manager (PDM) simplifies this whole process by giving you the entry, compile, and call options on the same screen that lists your source members. The AS/400 encourages the use of libraries, which go at the beginning of your program.

```
#include <stdio.h>
#include <xyz/names>
#include "ghi/funcs"
```

The first #include above searches for a source file named "H" in the C library, QCC. Then within that file, it looks for a member called "STDIO." That sounds pretty complicated, but the results you expect will happen. The second #include, using AS/400 format, looks in QCC for a file called NAMES and a member in it called XYZ. These two forms are interchangeable. The third, because of the enclosing quotes, looks in a user library instead of QCC. It will include a file called FUNCS and a member in it called GHI. This distinction is important when you want to include your own source code.

DATA FORMATS

Character data is 1 byte long. That is a comfortable length, but the AS/400 uses EBCDIC, not ASCII coding. As long as you just use characters as characters, they will be compatible with ASCII machines' programs. But do not expect to add 10 to "A" to get "K." EBCDIC is not arranged like that. Or if you have hard coded a numeric value for a character, like 65 for "A," you will have trouble.

All multi-byte AS/400 fields are laid out from left to right, from the byte with the lowest address to the byte with the highest address. Short integers are 2 bytes long, and long ones are 4. They both begin at the left with the sign bit. Programs based upon special knowledge of a specific implementation may have trouble on the AS/400. If, on the other hand, the programs are written in proper C form, it should be fine.

Float numbers are 4 bytes, and double numbers are 8. These IEEE standard format numbers are different from most other machines. Unless you use pieces of floating point numbers, that will not cause a problem. Actually the IEEE format is quite good. Short integers give about 9 digits of precision with a range from power(10, –38) to power(10, 38). Doubles give about 17 digits of precision with a range from power(10, –308) to power(10, 308).

AS/400 pointers are 16 bytes long. You cannot manipulate them with anything other than normal pointer operations. The system sees to that by using tag bits that you cannot access because they are out of the machine's addressing scheme. If you try assigning a non-pointer number to a pointer, the pointer will no longer be a pointer. If you try to use it, the system will stop your program.

Pointers cannot be stored on disk, so reading a "pointer" from a file is invalid. The system is not just being fussy about these restrictions. It keeps tasks from interfering with one another by keeping control of pointers. Further, the system storage manager may assign your program different addresses each time it runs, so a stored pointer would probably point to the wrong information anyway. You can, however, save offsets from a pointer. Then when you need them, read them from disk and base them on a valid pointer.

The AS/400 has no registers accessible by user programs, so the register storage class operates at the same speed as other storage.

Your program may allocate storage space and load data into it with the intent that it will be available quickly whenever an operator needs it. The AS/400's storage management will interfere with that plan. If any task running in your storage pool needs memory, the AS/400 will steal the least recently used pages of memory for it. If your program has not referenced the data lately, the AS/400 may write parts or all of your table on disk temporarily and give away your storage. When eventually your program refers to the table, the AS/400 will retrieve it from disk. Everything works fine, but probably not as quickly as you had in mind.

C structures should be watched. The AS/400, except for pointers, has no boundary alignment requirements. Any kind of field can start on any byte. On the other hand, C requires data to be defined on boundaries. For instance, if the first two variables you define in a structure are a short and long integer, C will put a 2-byte pad between them to make the long integer begin on a 4-byte boundary. As long as C is the only language involved, the structure will be fine.

Suppose an RPG III program defines a 2-byte and a 4-byte integer. There would be no space between them; RPG has no boundary alignment requirements. Next, the RPG program writes the numbers to a data file, and a C program reads that file. C expects a short, a 2-byte pad between the short and long integer. The C program will run, but not successfully.

SAA standards provide a packed-structure definition that makes C define structures like other languages, as in the example below. The definition is needed only when mixing data from different languages.

```
_packed struct example{
                     short    x;
                     int      y;
                     };
```

C doesn't handle decimal data, but it has conversion routines you can use. These routines convert between integer or double and packed or zoned data. They are named to describe their operations, such as Zoned TO Double and Packed TO Double, etc. The names start with "QXX," followed by a 4-character abbreviation of their function:

```
ZTOD (Zoned TO Double)
ZTOI (Zoned TO Integer)
DTOZ (Double TO Zoned)
ITOZ (Integer TO Zoned)
PTOD (Packed TO Double)
PTOI (Packed TO Integer)
DTOP (Double TO Packed)
ITOP (Integer TO Packed)
```

Packed and zoned data are the same as that used by the commercial languages RPG III and COBOL. Zoned has one digit in each byte. Packed puts two digits in each byte except the rightmost one, which has one digit and the sign.

DISK FILES

The AS/400 likes to create database files and usually keeps that privilege for itself. However, C/400 can create files. If MYFILE doesn't exist, C/400 creates it with a record length of 25 bytes. If MYFILE does exist, C/400 clears it.

```
fp = fopen("MYFILE","wb lrecl=25")
```

Binary record files are normal AS/400 database files. Binary stream files, on the other hand, are simulated using normal AS/400 database files, as in the above example. The AS/400 holds your stream data until it has a full record, then writes it. It will even write or read across record boundaries to make AS/400 records look like a stream. You need to be careful about the end of file, though. The AS/400 file management system keeps track only of whole records in closed files. If your stream ends in the middle of a record (as it probably will), the AS/400 loses track of the record end-of-file marker when you close the file. If you open the file later for input, the end-of-file marker will not be found until the end of the record that holds your last data is reached. Also, if you open the file to add more data to it, the new data will start in a new record, and there will be a gap between the last of your old data and the start of the new.

Text stream files are AS/400 source files. Each new line character sent causes the remaining bytes of the AS/400 record to be blanked and the whole record written. On a READ, blanks at the end of a disk record are interpreted as a new line character. For most applications this works fine, but you should know that if you send "ABC   \n" you will get "ABC\n" in return.

While stream file access is not available to commercial languages, the AS/400 makes it available to C programs. Other languages can process these files; they do not have stream access methods. C binary record files map perfectly to AS/400 database files. You can even take advantage of external file descriptions. In the following example, "both" means that you will be both reading and writing the records when accessing external database data definitions; "p z" tells data management to pass packed and zoned data in character fields.

```
#pragma mapinc("template","MASTFILE(ITMREC)","both","p z")
#include "template"
```

The compiler directives in the example above access the definitions of the ITMREC record within the file MASTFILE. It assures that your source definitions agree with the file and lets your program automatically pickup definition changes just by recompiling. The #include puts the data definitions in your program as if you had written:

```
typdef  struct  {
  char  NBR[3];
  char  NAME[15];
  char  AMT[4];
}MASTFILE_ITMREC_both_t;
```

The AS/400 is excellent at sharing its resources and files among many operators, and it protects one operator from another by file locking. Most languages' file definitions tell the system exactly what kind of operations a program will be performing. C, on the other hand, presents special problems with its rather simple file definitions and flexible operations. To protect other operators, the AS/400 must "assume the worst" from any program accessing a disk file. The result is that two people may not be able to run programs at the same time when they access the same file. For instance, only one stream I/O program at a time can access a file. Record I/O, on the other hand is more easily shared.

STANDARD WORKSTATION INPUT AND OUTPUT

The AS/400 provides a format and file to be used by stdin, stdout, and stderr. Actually, it is the same format used by BASIC. If you run a BASIC program, then run a C program, you may see some of your old BASIC data again. A Control Language (CL) command, RCLRSC, issued between the programs will clear the buffer.

The stdin/stdout/stderr format has an input line at the bottom of the screen, and output scrolls up from there. The format lets you use the up/down arrow keys to scroll through old output. The input line can be extended by pressing function key 21, and you can retrieve old input by pressing function key 9 to save yourself from keying it in again. Since the AS/400 has separate processors to handle individual workstation keystrokes, unbuffered I/O is impossible. On the AS/400, fully buffered and line-buffered I/O are the same.

AS/400 Workstation Files

The typical workstation (or display) file has two buffers and optionally a third. One buffer holds all of the variable data to be written. The second holds all of the variable data that was read. Display files use indicators to control their functions and pass certain operator actions back to your program. An indicator is a single character with the value of "1" or "0" for on or off, respectively. By default, these are at the beginning of each buffer.

Since C programmers often map their own fields in the display file buffers, cosmetic changes to display file definitions that add or remove indicators can require corresponding changes to your data definitions. A Data Description Specification (DDS) for display files permits you to pass your indicators in a separate buffer. Since there are 99 numeric indicators, you can make this a 99-character buffer, and no data definition changes will be needed as you add or subtract indicators. The DDS word is INDARA. Put that at the top of your file's DDS, and the third buffer will be set aside. A C macro, _Rindara, will set up the indicator buffer in your program.

To help you with the two data buffers, the listing from a DDS "compilation" gives you their layouts. The display file does most of the work to make the screen look attractive. It can suppress leading zeros, insert commas, decimal points, dollar signs, etc. It positions the fields on the screen and assigns attributes such as color, intensity, underscore, or blink.

The basic process is to select the display file format with:

```
QXXFORMAT("FORMAT1    ")
```

This selects a format called FORMAT1. Then use fwrite and fread to perform record I/O. All subsequent fwrites and freads will use FORMAT1 until you select a new format.

COMMUNICATIONS

Communications is very similar to workstation operations. The Intersystem Communication Function (ICF) takes most of the difficulty out of communications programming. You have two data buffers, an optional indicator buffer, and formats to select just like display files. A simple communications program may be identical to one with a display file.

The biggest difference between display and communications files is that errors are likely in communications, so recovery code is generally included. ICF keeps the program informed about how things are going through major/minor return codes in fields called major_ret_code and minor_ret_code. You will find a pointer to these is in the I/O feedback area.

All files have I/O feedback areas to give you information about them, but most file instructions are written with all the information they need. With communications, that is different. For instance, the program tells the system which file to access for a database file. However, in communications, the program may not know what city or terminal may be calling or even the terminal type, etc. The I/O feedback area has that information.

You will find major/minor return code documentation in the ICF manual. Basically, you want zeros. The documentation tells you what to do when the return codes are not zeros. Should you retry? Should you reacquire the terminal? Should you close and open the file? Should you give up? The answers are there. As a programmer, you need to decide what degree of recovery to include in your program.

RUNNING A C PROGRAM

Programs are stored in AS/400 libraries by their names. Since most languages support single entry points, a program name corresponds to an entry point. When you call program X, the machine searches the library directory for X, loads it, and branches to entry point X.

If the main C program calls entry point Y in program Z, the system will look for program Y in the library and will not find it. Program Z is there, but how can the system know that entry point Y is in program Z?

That problem is solved by CL command SETPGMINF (set program information). Its parameters name the main program and all other programs needed to run. This command attaches these names to the main program so that it will know where to look for any call.

When you call the main program, all of the needed programs will be accessed and a table will be built of all entry points along with the names of the programs they are in. So there will be no more mystery. When you call Y, the machine knows to get Z for you.

All C programs have a program information table attached. . .even if you do not use SETPGMINF. These default tables point to the C library so that for simple programs, you do not need SETPGMINF.

When you call the main program, the AS/400 builds an environment. As long as the main program is active, subsequent calls to C programs will run in that same environment. That means they can share global data and reach each other with longjmp. When the main C program ends, so does its environment. Calling CL, RPG, and COBOL programs does not interfere with an environment; the programs will not know it exists.

Non-C programs can call C entry points (other than the main program) with the help of another program. That program, QPXXCALL, identifies the entry point, the program that contains it, a name to give the environment, and up to 32 parameters for the program. Because you know its name, you can run several C programs in the environment:

```
CALL QPXXCALL('y', 'MYENVIR', 'Z', RETURN)
```

If you finish with your environment, another program, QPXXDLTE, will delete it. Actually C programs can use QPXXCALL, too. The result is an additional environment with only the passed parameters in common and no shared global definitions.

DEBUGGING

The AS/400 includes a debugger that gives you access to running compiled programs that you would normally expect only of interpreted programs. C, with its multiple entry points, recursion, data scoping, and indirect references, would benefit little from the standard debugger. The C/400 debugger is started automatically when you look at C programs.

Use the normal STRDBG (start debug) command and ADDTRC (add trace) as you would for programs in other languages. When you start the program, the AS/400 debugger starts the special C debugger. It immediately asks you what to do.

You can tell the debugger where to put breakpoints in your programs and what data to display or change. When the data is referenced indirectly (maybe by a pointer that points to a pointer, which points to the data), you can enter the necessary C statement to reach it.

SUMMARY

The language of choice for programming the AS/400 is RPG III. While RPG had a rather limited origin that gave it an extremely restricted format, its subsequent developers have given it a flexibility and power well beyond anything its roots suggest. Even in a powerful, interactive, database system such as the AS/400,

RPG III is a powerful tool for development of commercial programs that take advantage of the system's capabilities and speed. And RPG has proven easy to learn and easy to write.

RPG III is a friendly member of the AS/400 language family. It can call any other programming language, and any other language can call an RPG III program. The AS/400 has a standard CALL interface for all languages, and there are compatible data formats so that parameters can be passed and received.

Do not worry if you discover a few dinosaur bones in the language such as stacker selection of punched cards, zone moves, or forcing input. They should give you a sense of history, and if they are still supported in your system, they may give you a creative solution to a tricky problem.

While there are several other languages you can use on the AS/400, RPG is generally the language of choice. RPG programmers can always find experts to answer their questions, which is not true for other languages. One should not conclude that RPG is necessarily the best AS/400 language, but it is the most popular and for many good reasons.

C/400 is a very flexible language that lets you perform operations not possible with other languages such as RPG. For most commercial operations (accessing the database, decimal arithmetic, workstation and communications operations, etc.) other languages can get as "close" to the machine as C can. All AS/400 languages work effectively with multiple operators running the same program. As a result, the reasons for choosing C/400 are few. Clearly, migrating existing C applications to the AS/400 is one of the strongest reasons. Occasionally, there may be applications needing number crunching or text parsing. If these represent a significant part of a program's work, then C may be a good choice. Of course, if C is your language of choice, you will want to use it.

8

Security

Se-cu-ri-ty 1. The quality or state of being secure: as a: freedom from danger: SAFETY b: freedom from fear or anxiety c: freedom from want or deprivation <job~>.
Webster's Ninth New Collegiate Dictionary (Springfield, MA: Merriam-Webster Inc., 1991)

Security for a computer installation can mean many things. A system that is critical to the operation of a business must protect against unauthorized use or unauthorized access to business information. The system should be protected in the event of a disaster such as fire, flood, earthquake, vandalism, and a host of conditions that may result in the destruction of the system, the data it contains, or both. While all of these topics may be considered under the topic of security, the discussion in this chapter deals with security on a system that is operating in a normal physical environment and where the use of the system is shared by a variety of users with varying needs for access to the system and the data stored on the system.

Concerns for security involve the use of the resources on the system. Specific resources should be available to those who have a legitimate need for the resources and should be denied to those who do not have access to the specific resources. The AS/400 controls access by identifying each user of the system by means of a user profile name and using that name to authorize users to system resources.

The AS/400 is quite articulate about the use of systems resources. Many of the resources are defined as objects and each object is a specific object type. A program is defined as object type *PGM, a file is object type *FILE, and a device such as a magnetic tape drive is object type *DEVD. There are more than 60 object types, and the operations that may be performed upon each type are defined by the AS/400 operating system. A certain measure of security is provided by restricting operations based on object type. A program (*PGM) object, for example, is intended to be used to perform computer instructions. A program cannot be treated as data; therefore it cannot be read as a file and altered. Programs on PCs and many other computer systems can be treated as data files, thus the programs can be altered. A computer virus is a program that can reproduce itself by altering other programs that continue to propagate the virus. The AS/400 prevents viruses and other intrusions into the system through a combination of "object-oriented architecture" and an strict definition of user authorizations. Object-oriented architecture uses an addressing technique called capability-based addressing, which essentially means that objects can be accessed by name only, not by address. Programs cannot find items via a computer address as on other architectures. Because the system requires access by name, the system at a hardware level checks the authority of the intended user against the security of the object before allowing access to the object. Thus the AS/400 provides a strong base for a granular and comprehensive authorization scheme that relates objects and their allowed functions to the users of the system.

LEVELS OF SECURITY

While the AS/400 provides a tightly controlled security environment, it is not necessary to implement full security. If your situation does not warrant a comprehensive design for security, there is no cause for alarm. The system is shipped from IBM with essentially no security and you can continue to operate it without security controls. Security at a global level is defined by one of four levels of security, ranging from no security to one in which all system resources are tightly secured. The system is shipped with the system value QSECURITY at 10, no security. The four levels represented by their QSECURITY values are listed below.

Level	*Description*
10	The system is unsecured. Anyone can use it. The AS/400 is shipped at this level of security.
20	Users must sign on with a password. No other security applies.
30	Resources are secured. A user must sign on with a password and then can access only the objects to which he or she is authorized.
40	The system is secured as in level 30 with added protection against the use of unsupported system interfaces.

The global security level at which your system operates is defined by a system value. The name of that system value is QSECURITY and is changed by the change system value command, CHGSYSVAL. The following command results in a system that is resource secured at level 30.

```
CHGSYSVAL QSECURITY('30')
```

Security levels 10 and 20 are breifly described in the following two paragraphs. Most of the remainder of this section describes security at level 30 and then ends with the additional security features provided at level 40.

LEVEL 10

Security level 10 allows anyone to use a workstation. A user can type a user name on a workstation and press Enter. If that user name is not known to the system, the system will create a user by that name and allow the user full access to everything on the system. For systems where the only security needed is access to a workstation and that security is provided by the facilities that house the system and its workstations, level 10 is adequate security.

LEVEL 20

Security level 20 is much like level 10 except that user names are defined in the system by an authorized security officer or administrator. A password is associated with each user. A user must type in a user name and the associated password in order to gain access to the system. After a successful sign-on, the user has full access to the system.

LEVEL 30

Security level 30 requires each user to sign on to the system using the password associated with the user's name. Upon successfully signing on, the user is able to access only those objects to which the user is authorized. Level 30 is often called resource security. A user signed on in this way is identified by a "user profile name" associated with a user profile object, *USRPRF, which is used to determine the authority of the user on the system.

A user profile object must be created beforehand for each user. The profiles are normally created by either the user designated as the Security Officer or by some other user who has been given special security administration authority. Suppose a user profile is created for Mary. The name of the user profile object carries the name of the user, thus the object is named MARY. A wealth of information is stored as part of the functional part of the user profile, including the password for the user, a list of objects that the user owns (initially this is an empty list), the objects to which the user has been granted authority, information for routing printed output, and much more. An important piece of information in the user profile determines what happens after the user correctly enters a password to sign on to the system. There are two entries in the profile that control the initial startup for the user. They control whether the user will see a menu on the workstation screen or whether the user will immediately begin running a specific program. One entry is the name of an initial program and the other is the name of an initial menu. If both an initial program and an initial menu are specified, then the initial program is chosen as the starting point. This starting point marks the first work associated with this job.

The term job is used to define the work that a user begins at sign-on time. The job ends when the user signs off or when the system causes the job to end for some other reason. All access to objects on the system is made by way of program requests for functions. Programs must always run within a job environment associated with a user profile. Consequently, access to objects is controlled by a combination of the access attempted by the program and the authorities granted to the user profile associated with the job.

What kind of authorities does a user have to individual objects? That is a central question that will be addressed in the following paragraphs. The answer, in part, is that the authorities that can be granted to a user are dependent upon the type of object.

Object Authorization

Let's begin by talking about a *FILE object. A file is an object that contains data. The kinds of operations that programs need to perform upon a data file are to read the data, change the data, write new data, and delete existing data items. The authority to operate on the data within a file is identified as "data rights" and the four data rights are *READ, *UPDATE, *ADD, and *DELETE. Not all users who use the file should have the authority to perform all four of these functions, however. The AS/400 provides a granular approach to data files that allows any individual user to be authorized to any combination of these four functions. Consider three users who work with payroll data. Mary has the responsibility of entering new employees into the payroll file, so she needs to be able to add new employee records to the file. Jim handles changes to names, addresses, and salaries such as promotions and pay raises. Jim needs to be able

PAYROLL File				
User Profile Name	Data Rights			
	*READ	*ADD	*UPD	*DLT
MARY		X		
JIM	X		X	
SUE	X	X	X	X

Figure 8.1 Data rights to the payroll file

to read and update records in the file. Sue has overall supervisory responsibilities and needs to be able to read, add, update, and delete records from the file. A chart of the data rights to the payroll file is shown in Figure 8.1.

The granting of these authorities (or rights) is accomplished by means of a command, the grant object authority command, GRTOBJAUT. The following example shows the granting of authority for Sue.

```
GRTOBJAUT OBJ(PAYROLL) OBJTYPE(*FILE) USER(SUE) +
AUT(*READ *ADD *UPD *DLT)
```

Note: The command would ordinarily be listed on a single line. The + at the end of the first line indicates that the command is continued on the next line.

Object Rights

The example above illustrates the granular level of security that can be applied to data. What about security for other objects such as programs? The answer is that another set of object rights control access to the object as a whole. These three object rights apply to all objects including data: They are operational, management, and existence rights.

Operational rights grant the authority to perform basic operations upon the object. For programs this means the authority to run the program. For files it means the authority to open the file. For all other objects it simply means the authority to use the object for its intended use.

Existence rights means that the user with this authority can delete the object. This authority is quite different from the delete authority applied to data. The data right refers to the authority to delete individual records in a file. Existence rights apply to the authority to delete the entire object.

Management rights refer to the authority to manage the object in the following ways. The object can be renamed, authorities can be granted or revoked up

PAYROLL File							
User	-- Object Rights -			----- Data Rights -----			
Profile Name	*OPR	*MGT	*EXIST	*READ	*ADD	*UPD	*DLT
MARY	X				X		
JIM	X			X		X	
SUE	X			X	X	X	X

Figure 8.2 Adding rights to the PAYROLL file

to but not exceeding the authorities of the user performing the management function, and the object can be moved to another library.

After adding these rights to the PAYROLL file in the earlier example, the chart looks like Figure 8.2.

Objects also have owners, and owners have all rights to the objects they own. If Wes is the owner of this object, the chart would look like Figure 8.3.

This chart indicates that Wes has all object rights and all data rights. Wes can change the name of the file from PAYROLL to some other name because he has management (*MGT) rights. He could also delete the entire file because he has existence (*EXIST) rights to the object.

We now know the authorities that Mary, Jim, Sue, and Wes have to the Payroll file. What about everyone else? Is there some way of identifying public rights for all other users on the system? The answer is yes, via *PUBLIC authority. The name *PUBLIC is treated as a special user name. If the public is excluded from the payroll file (the public has no authority to the file) the chart looks like Figure 8.4.

Notice that in this example none of the columns for *PUBLIC contains an X to indicate authority. If public authority were appropriate for this file, the appropriate authorities could be granted for *PUBLIC and Xs would be shown in the appropriate columns.

PAYROLL File							
User	-- Object Rights -			----- Data Rights -----			
Profile Name	*OPR	*MGT	*EXIST	*READ	*ADD	*UPD	*DLT
MARY	X				X		
JIM	X			X		X	
SUE	X			X	X	X	X
WES	X	X	X	X	X	X	X

Figure 8.3 Object owner has all object and data rights

PAYROLL File							
User	Object Rights			Data Rights			
Profile Name	*OPR	*MGT	*EXIST	*READ	*ADD	*UPD	*DLT
MARY	X				X		
JIM	X			X		X	
SUE	X			X	X	X	X
WES	X	X	X	X	X	X	X
*PUBLIC							

Figure 8.4 *PUBLIC as user name

Certain combinations of authorities have been given shortcut definitions. These are defined as *ALL, *CHANGE, *USE, and *EXCLUDE. Figure 8.5 shows how they are displayed. Notice that combinations that do not fit these definitions are shown as USER DEF (user defined).

Group Profiles

Authorities can be granted using the special names of *ALL, *CHANGE, *USE, and *EXCLUDE to simplify the stating of authorities. The examples up to this point have illustrated the granular nature of AS/400 security. Using this approach a system can be tightly controlled so that each individual user has exactly the authority that is required to carry out the user's responsibilities.

In the real world of computing, one frequently finds that the functions such as those defined for Jim in Figure 8.4 are not the responsibility of a single individual. A group of people or perhaps a whole department will share in like responsibilities. Would it not be useful to define the authorities once for the

PAYROLL File								
User		Object Rights			Data Rights			
Profile Name		*OPR	*MGT	*EXIST	*READ	*ADD	*UPD	*DELETE
Rose	*ALL	X	X	X	X	X	X	X
Wes	*CHANGE	X			X	X	X	X
Cheryl	*USE	X			X			
Hank	*EXCLUDE							
Sue	USER DEF	X	X		X	X	X	

Figure 8.5 Shortcut definitions

group or the department and then associate the individual users with the group in such a way as to allow each member of the group to take on the authorities of the group? An AS/400 group profile provides that capability. A group profile is given the authority needed for a group of users. Individual users are identified as members of the group, and each member takes on the same set of authorities as the group, provided that individual authorities do not have differing authorities that override the authorities of the group profile.

Group profiles can greatly simplify authority management, especially if naming conventions are adopted that provide positive identification of group profiles. The AS/400 allows any valid name to be used as a group profile, so the responsibility of defining a meaningful standard rests with the system administrator. Using names like GRPxxx or DEPTxxx, where the first letters of the name clearly identify the profile as a group profile, is one example. It should be noted that there is nothing in a user profile that identifies it as a group profile. The deciding factor is that the member profiles reference the user profile as the group profile. Members are added to a group by identifying the group name in the individual profile. The individual user is thereby given immediate authority that is identical to the authority of the group profile, provided that the individual profile does not have authorities that override the authorities of the group. Individual authorities always take precedence over the authorities associated with the group and completely replace the authorities associated with the group. For example, suppose user profile JIM is a member of group profile DEPT502. DEPT502 has all data rights to the file PAYROLL. JIM is given read and update authority to PAYROLL. The result is that JIM has read and update authority because of individual authorities, but he does not have the additional authorities of add and delete that are associated with the group. That is to say that the individual authorities are used in place of the group authorities and group authorities for individual objects cannot be added to individual authorities.

In Figure 8.6, DEPT502 has authorities to a program and two files.

Individual profiles ROSE and CHERYL are members of group profile DEPT502. ROSE has been granted *USE authority to library ROSELIB, and CHERYL has been granted *READ authority to the file PAYF. The net result for ROSE and CHERYL is shown in Figure 8.7.

```
A        *PGM      *USE
NAMEF    *FILE     *ALL
PAYF     *FILE     *CHANGE
```

Figure 8.6 Group profile DEPT502 authorities

```
ROSE
A          *PGM    *USE      (from the group profile)
NAMEF      *FILE   *ALL      (from the group profile)
PAYF       *FILE   *CHANGE   (from the group profile)
ROSELIB    *LIB    *USE      (individual authority)
```

Figure 8.7a Profile ROSE

```
CHERYL
A          *PGM    *USE      (from the group profile)
NAMEF      *FILE   *ALL      (from the group profile)
PAYF       *FILE   *READ     (individual authority)
```

Figure 8.7b Profile CHERYL

Notice that ROSE acquired all of the authorities of the group profile and has additional authority to the library named ROSELIB. CHERYL acquired the authorities of the group except for the authority to file PAYF, where individual authhority overrides the group authority to PAYF. In this example, the authority has been reduced as a result of the reduced individual authority.

Group profiles exist at a single level only. A group profile cannot be a member of yet another group, and a user can be a member of only one group. Consequently, when an individual profile specifies a new group profile, the member loses its prior group identity and becomes a member of a new group. Helpful guidelines for dividing users into groups can be found in the *AS/400: Basic Security Guide*, SC41-0047 manual. Additional detail is given in the *AS/400: Security Reference*, SC41-8083 manual.

Ordinarily when a user creates an object such as a program or a file, the user who creates it owns it. When the user is the member of a group, however, the ownership can either be given to the creator or to the group profile. When the choice is to give ownership to the user, then a second choice is available. The second choice is what authorities (if any) are given to the group profile. A consideration to bear in mind when contemplating giving ownership to the group profile is that it is not possible to determine after the fact which user created the object.

On systems that have multiple users, the use of group profiles is highly advisable. As new users are added to departments or functional areas, they can be made a member of the appropriate group profile and immediately acquire the authorities needed. With careful planning, it may be possible to avoid giving individual authorities.

Maintaining control over security is simplified and security audits are much easier when group profiles are used and authorities are given to the group rather than to individuals. More information about auditing and other recommendations is forthcoming after some additional features of AS/400 security have been explained.

OBJECT STRUCTURE

Object structure and the way objects are secured must be understood in order to make the most efficient use of the system. The next few paragraphs explain the security-related features of object structure and its relationship to the use of public authority and authorization lists.

The first point to understand is that object structure has a fixed format and a limited amount of storage for object information. Since any number of users can be individually authorized to use an object, the object structure cannot accommodate a variable number of names and authorities in its structure. The method used by the AS/400 is to associate the objects with the user profile rather than to associate the users with the object.

Consequently, the user profile lists the objects to which the user is authorized and the type of authorization that applies. The object structure is examined first. The object contains information such as the object name, object type, date of creation, date last saved, etc. In addition the following information related to security is contained in the object description:

Object owner (user profile name)
Public access
Authorization list name

When an object is saved to tape or diskette, the security information listed above is saved with the object. The information in the user profile that lists the objects the user is authorized to use is not saved. Furthermore, if an object is deleted after it is saved, all references to its authority are removed from all user profiles that were granted authority to it. What this means in practical terms is that if an object is saved, then deleted and subsequently restored, all individual authorities from the original copy of the object are lost. They are not restored along with the object. Only the three items listed above (the owner, public access, and authorization list name) are restored because they are part of the object structure that is saved and restored as part of the object. Authorization lists provide a solution to this potential problem and offer some additional

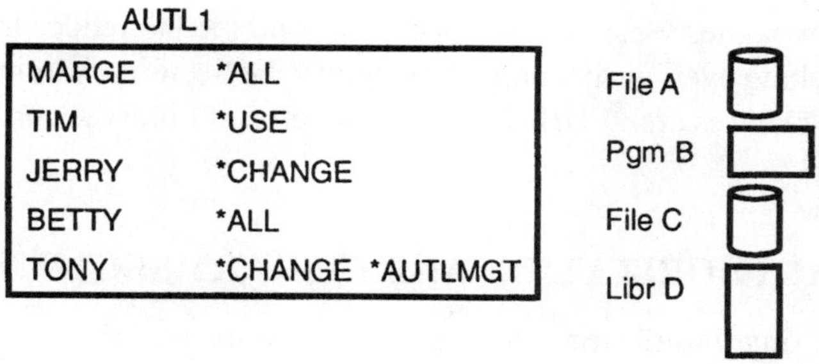

Figure 8.8 Authorization Lists

advantages to the Security Administrator. A key advantage is that the authorization is part of the standard object description that is saved and restored with the object.

Figure 8.8 illustrates an authorization list named AUTL1 and the objects it secures. The authorization list specifies authorities for five user profiles: Marge, Tim, Jerry, Betty, and Tony and is used to secure the objects shown to the right of the list.

AUTHORIZATION LISTS

An authorization list names users and authorities associated with each user. When an object names the list, all users and the associated authorities from the list are used to secure the object. Any number of authorization lists can be created, but an object can name only one authorization list. A Security Administrator can define a set of users and related authorities and then secure any number of objects with the list. It is much easier to secure an object by naming a single authorization list rather than securing each object using each of the profile names. New objects can be secured quickly if an existing authorization list is used that provides the required protection. When a user is removed from a list, the removal affects all objects secured by that list.

Since the AS/400 checks the security of objects before allowing their use, it is wise to use techniques that allow an efficient means of checking security. The use of authorization lists can significantly reduce the number of authorization entries associated with user profiles, thereby reducing the time the system spends finding the appropriate authorizations. By combining the use of group profiles and authorization lists, the number of authorizations in user profiles is further reduced. Fortunately, combining these two techniques is a win/win proposition. It makes security administration easier and at the same time more efficient.

Two other security features can be combined to reduce the amount of security checking even further and also simplify the Security Administrator's task. These two features are *PUBLIC authorization and library security.

PUBLIC AUTHORIZATION AND LIBRARY SECURITY

Securing libraries first, then arranging for the security of objects within secured libraries can further simplify security administration and speed up the security checking process at the same time. For libraries that should be accessed by a small set of users (specified via group profiles if possible), it is wise to specify a public (*PUBLIC) authority to *EXCLUDE the public from the library. Having done that, the only users who are allowed access to objects within the library should be named in an authorization list, and that authorization list should then be used to secure the library. Turning attention to the objects within the library relieves the Security Administrator of concerns about users who have been excluded from the library. The Administrator can grant "public" authority to objects within the library. "Public" in this context takes on a new meaning by referring to only those users who have access to the library. Public authorities can be granted to the objects in a way that relates to the majority of users who have access to the library. Each object that requires additional security is secured by an authorization list that names group profile names. This combination maximizes the use of authorities directly defined by the object and minimizes the number of authorities that are associated with the user profiles.

Public authorization information and an authorization list name are stored in the object description and are saved and restored with the object. Whenever possible, use public security to secure an object and handle exceptions with an authorization list.

Authorization lists have one more security feature that is unique to authorization lists, *AUTLMGT authority. Authorization list management authority may be granted to a user, who then has the rights to change the authorities of users named in the authorization list. Notice in Figure 8.8 that Tony has authorization list management rights along with *CHANGE rights. Authorization list management rights allow Tony to add or remove names on the list with rights less than or up to the *CHANGE level of security. Tony can change the authorities on the list for users with less than or equal to his own authority, but he cannot give authority greater than *CHANGE nor reduce the authority of anyone having authority greater than *CHANGE. Thus Tony cannot change the authority of Marge or Betty, but he can raise the authority of Tim to *CHANGE or remove some or all of Tim's authority.

Based on the information given up to this point, it is possible to make several recommendations for implementing security on an AS/400:

1. Determine which groups of users will perform the same functions and establish group profiles for each group. Be sure to use a naming convention that will clearly distinguish group profiles from other profiles. The reason for this will become more evident in the discussion of auditing considerations. Specify PASSWORD(*NONE) for the password associated with the group profile. This reserves the profile for reference use only because no password exists for the profile. The security officer can change the profile, if necessary, to provide a password when maintenance work needs to be done using the group profile. When the maintenance activity is completed, the password can be changed back to *NONE.
2. Plan library usage to include separation of objects on the basis of whom should have access to them. If the library should not be available to the public users on the system, then set the public access to *EXCLUDE and use an authorization list to grant authority to the appropriate group profiles. Use that authorization list to secure the library.
3. For each object in a library, determine the level of usage required by most users who have access to the library. Set the public authorization to that level of usage.
4. Handle exceptions to 3 above by establishing authorization lists to secure the objects. Use group profile names to provide security in as many instances as possible. Use individual authorities sparingly to handle exceptions. If individual authorities are needed frequently, consider establishing one or more additional group profiles to provide the needed security.

AUTHORIZATION SEARCH ORDER

The recommendations made earlier are based on the order in which the AS/400 checks for security. If all of the recommendations given earlier are followed, then it should not be difficult to determine what level of authority is given to each user. Since it is possible to specify authority at several places, which may not all agree, it is helpful to know the order in which the AS/400 checks the authorizations in order to determine the actual authority given to a user for a specific object. Figure 8.9 shows the components of the authorization search. It is important to understand that as the system searchs for authority, it does not

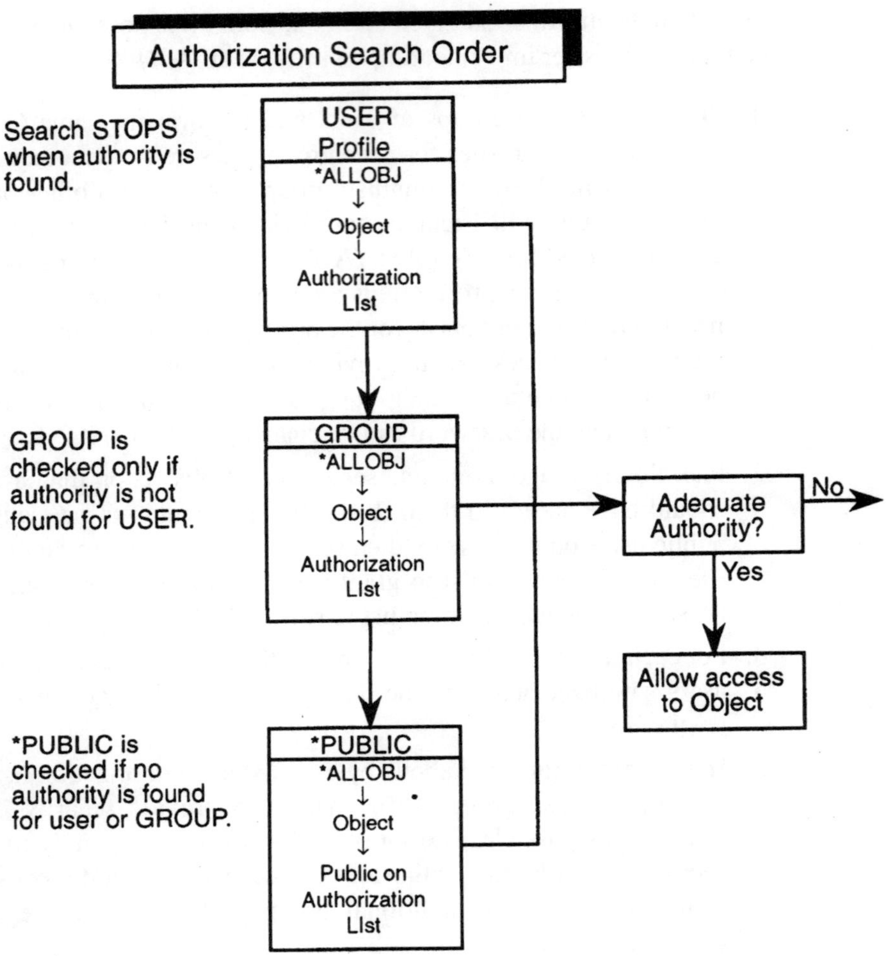

Figure 8.9 Authorization List Management

look for adequate authority to end the search. It looks for any statement of authority and stops the search when it finds one. Security checking starts at the top left of the figure with a test for authority granted to the individual user. That authority, if stated, will be found in the user profile. The first statement the AS/400 looks for is whether the user has been granted all authority via the *ALLOBJ value. If so, the search ends and the user has authority to anything on the system. If *ALLOBJ was not specified for the user, then the system checks for specific authority granted to the user. If the user was granted *EXCLUDE authority, that counts as specific authority for the user. If the system finds specific authority for the user, then the search stops. If the AS/400 has not found a statement of authorization, it next checks whether the object names an authorization list. If an authorization list is named for the object, the system checks the list for an authorization statement for this user. If an authorization is found (even if the statement is *EXCLUDE), then the search stops. At this point the system has checked everything that pertains to the user. If it still has not found an authorization statement, it will check for exactly the same statements, except that it will look for them in relation to the group of which this user is a member. If the user is not a member of a group, then of course the group authorization checking is skipped. The next step is to look for public authorization, and there are only two places to look. The system looks first at the object itself. If it finds no public authorization statement, it looks for a public authorization statement in the authorization list (if there is one) named by the object.

If after checking all three possible places for authorization nothing is found, then the user is denied addressability (access) to the requested object.

If the system did find an authorization statement, then the system determines whether the stated authorization is adequate for the function being requested. For example, a program attempts to open a file for update. In order to open the file, the user must have operational rights to the file object. In order to update records, the user must have read and update rights to the data. If all of these rights are included in the user's authorization, then the system determines that the authority it found is adequate and the system opens the file and makes it available to the program. If the authority is inadequate, access may or may not be denied. The program that requested the object may specify that the user of the program will be granted the authority of the owner of the program while the program is active. These programs adopt the owner's authority.

ADOPTION OF AUTHORITY BY PROGRAMS

When a program is created, the create command can specify that the program will adopt the owner's authority. This is accomplished by the parameter USRPRF(*OWNER) associated with each command that creates a program. The default value is USRPRF(*USER), which means that the program does not adopt the owner's authority. This program adoption value can be changed later by either the security officer or the owner of the program via the CHGPGM command.

When programs adopt the owner's authority, the authorities of both the user and the owner are combined to provide the authority that is in effect. Contrast this with the earlier description of the authorization search order, where the system takes the first authorization statement it finds using the search order and ignores any other authorization statments that could provide a greater degree of authorization.

Adoption provides the system with a powerful security tool that permits a user's authority to be extended under program control. This can be valuable when a user needs to update a field in a record during the running of a program, but the user should not be allowed update ability outside the running of that program. The update will be completely controlled by the functions of the program that does the update, so the user will not have the ability to corrupt the file either intentionally or unintentionally. In this example the program would be owned by a profile that has update authority to the file in question and the program would adopt that owner's authority.

A word of caution is in order concerning program adoption. When a program that adopts the owner's authority calls another program, the called program carries forward the program adoption so the the owner's adopted authority remains in effect. It remains in effect as long as the program is active in the job (the program is in the job's program stack). A possible security exposure exists. Someone could write a new program with the same name as one called by a program that can adopt the owner's authority. Then the new program could be placed in a library that is ahead of the library that contains the old program of the same name. Consequently, the new program would be called instead.

Controlling a situation like this gets complicated and increases the difficulty of providing an effective security auditing procedure. Some installations where security is especially critical have decided to prohibit the use of programs that adopt authority and have put in place security audits that find and disable programs that adopt authority. Another less drastic method of control is to prohibit programs that adopt from calling other programs. Users who plan to use program adoption are advised to read the section on "Programs That Adopt the Owner's Authority" in *AS/400: Security Concepts and Planning*, SC41-8083.

SECURITY PERFORMANCE CONSIDERATIONS

Since the AS/400 checks an object before a user is allowed to use it, performance of the system is affected by the way security is implemented. The use of group profiles and authorization lists can significantly reduce the number of object security references stored with user profiles. Not only does this shorten the search time when the system establishes the level of authority of a user has to access an object, it also reduces the amount of storage needed to store security information and speeds up saves and subsequent restores of the system. When the system is saved or restored, user profiles and related information including security authorizations are also saved or restored. The authorizations stored in user profiles can be saved and restored in separate operations beginning with

AS/400 Version 2 Release 2.0. The SAVSECDTA command saves the authorities and the RSTAUT command restores them. The recommendations made earlier help to reduce the amount of information associated with user profiles. Consequently, less information is saved and restored so that the save and restore operations run more quickly.

The use of appropriate library lists can improve the performance of the authorization search process. When a library is placed in a user's library list, the system first checks to be sure that the user is authorized to use the library. When the authorization is established, the library is allocated to the user and placed in the user's library list. Allocating the library means that the system does not need to check the authority on the library again for subsequent references to objects within the library. Security checking is restricted to the object itself.

When library lists are not used to find objects, objects are referenced by providing both the library name and the object name. The system finds objects faster and performs security checking more efficiently when the library list is used to find the object rather than fully qualifying the user accessing both the library name and the object name.

Security Control Points

AS/400 security is controlled by means of three security control points. The first control point is through system values that have a global effect. System values were described earlier in this chapter. The second control point is through user profiles, and the third is object authority. The descriptions up to this point have concentrated mostly on object security and on the way that the user profile interacts with object security.

A considerable amount of information is associated with the user profile object. This chapter does not attempt to describe all the information in the user profile, but there are several items that are related to security. The items that are discussed in this section include passwords, special authorities, and user class.

Passwords

The password is an obvious and important part of security. Passwords associated with user profiles are encrypted and cannot be displayed, not even by the Security Officer. If a user forgets a password, it cannot be displayed. Consequently, the way to resolve the problem of a lost or forgotten password is for the Security Officer or someone with security administration authority to issue a new password for the user. User profiles are not required to have a password associated with them. A password of *NONE can be specified for a user profile. One reason for having user profiles without passwords is to use a profile as a group profile. All of the authorities needed by a group can be associated with a group profile that can only be used via profiles that are members of the group. The use of group profiles is strongly encouraged for systems needing high levels of security and having a moderate to large number of users.

Special Authorities

Special authorities are broadly associated with operational considerations. The *ALLOBJ (all object) special authority gives the profile authority to everything on the system. At system levels 10 and 20, all users have *ALLOBJ authority. That is the mechanism used to define a system that has either password security or no security. Other special authorities are security administration (*SECADM), save system (*SAVSYS), job control (*JOBCTL), service (*SERVICE), and spool control (*SPLCTL).

*SECADM special authority granted to a user profile gives that user the authority to enroll new users by creating new user profiles. *SECADM authority also allows changing passwords for any user. It carries with it the authority to enroll users in OfficeVision/400 and control the special authorities and access to office functions and office objects. This is a very powerful special authority and should be used with discretion.

*SAVSYS special authority allows a user with this attribute to save and restore the operating system and save and restore other objects on a system.

*JOBCTL special authority allows a user to control jobs on the system. This includes the authority to end jobs, hold them, release held jobs, and change some of the attributes associated with jobs such as changing the priority of a job that is running or that is on a job queue awaiting a chance to run.

*SERVICE is a special authority that is needed to run some of the diagnostic aids on the system. It is generally reservered for persons who service the hardware and software on the system.

*SPLCTL is a special authority that allows a user to manage the printers on the system. The user with this authority can start and stop spooled writers, delete spooled files, stop the printing of spooled files, hold spooled files, and release spooled files that were held.

User Class

User profiles have another value, user class, that can be used to give special authorities to user profiles. Valid user class values are *SECOFR, *SECADM,

*PGMR, *SYSOPR, and *USER. A user with user class *SECOFR is given all of the special authroities listed earlier. A user with *SECADM user class is given *SECADM, *SAVSYS, and JOBCTL special authorities. Users with *PGMR or *SYSOPR special authorities are given *SAVSYS and *JOBCTL special authorities. *USER user class is not given any special authorities. User class also provides another service—it controls which options are shown and usable from system menus.

Auditing Security

The system notes all rejections of attempted unauthorized access. A message noting the attempts, identifying the user, and identifying the object requested is sent to the history log, QHIST. This log therefore provides a minimal level of auditing. A more comprehensive auditing function is available by requesting that the system keep a journal of security events. The journal notes the use of or attempted use of restricted instructions, unsupported usage attempts, authorization requests that failed, objects that were deleted, and certain save and restore information.

SUMMARY

In this chapter, you have learned what security features are available on the AS/400 and how to implement them. The foundation for these features is how resources in the system are to be used and how access is provided to users. The AS/400 identifies users of the system by their user profiles and gives them varying levels of authorization to use system resources, based on their "need" as identified by their profiles. Security is also provided by restricting the operations that can be performed on many of the resources, which are defined as objects.

Four levels of security can be implemented by the System Adminstrator.

10—no security; anyone can use the system
20—password protection only
30—passwords are required of users for log-on; users can only access object types to which they have authorization
40—passwords; object authorizations; additional protection against unsupported system interfaces

The access rights, or authories, that can be granted to a user for an object depend upon the type of object. "Data rights" is the authority to perform operations upon data objects, such as the data found in a file. The four data rights are:

1. *READ (view data)
2. *UPD *update existing data)
3. *ADD (add new data)
4. *DLT (delete data)

"Object rights" is the authority to perform operations upon an object as a whole, such as a program. The three object rights are:

1. Operational rights—the authority to perform basic operations upon the object, such as running a program or opening a file.
2. Existence rights—the ability to delete the entire object, not just the data
3. Management rights—the right to rename objects, grant authorities to users at lesser levels of authority, and move objects

Shortcut authorities, which are certain combinations of the above authorities, can also be given to users instead of defining each individual right:

*ALL (all four data rights and all three object rights)
*CHANGE (existing authorities for a user are changed)
*USE (read and operational rights)
*EXCLUDE (no rights)

USER DEF is used for all other combinations of authorities. Public rights can be granted to all users of a specific library with the *PUBLIC authority. This same authority can be used to exclude public access to a library, by using *EXCLUDE.

Group profiles can simplify authority management. Authorities are assigned to a group profile, and individual users are assigned to a group and draw their access rights from it. Restrictions include that group profiles cannot be members of another group, and users can have only one group profile.

Another security feature is the object structure, which is a fixed format for limited information about an object, such as the object owner, object name, date of creation, public access, and authorization list name. An authorization list specifies authorities for each user in the list, which means users are not associated with objects.

Security can be implemented best by establishing group profiles for users who perform the same function, separating objects based on access needs, setting public authorization for objects based on level of usage for most users, and using authorization lists for exceptions to public access. Use of group profiles and authorization lists can improve performance of systems by reducing the number of object security references stored with user profiles.

Security is also controlled by three control points:

1. System values with a global effect
2. User profiles (including use of passwords, special authorities, and user class)
3. Object authority

9

Work Management

The objective of work management is to control the flow of work through the system, and on the AS/400, this concerns the means by which the AS/400 associates attributes to jobs. Those attributes determine which resources and how much of each resource the job is allowed to use during the time it is running. The programs themselves do not make the allocation of the resources; instead the programs run in a job environment that makes those determinations. Thus the same programs can be run concurrently in different jobs or at separate times with resource allocations tailored to the time and circumstances under which the programs are run.

The AS/400 is a multitasking system by design. The allocation of the systems resources determines how multiple tasks will compete with each other for limited resources to get the work done.

The topics in this chapter include an overview of work management structure and control, the means for managing this structure, and a suggested discipline for applying these controls to regulate work flow through the AS/400.

The AS/400 has tools, both automatic and user controlled, that allow you to "tune" the system for better performance. It is not necessary to know all the rules for tuning the system in order to get good performance. If, on the other hand, you have a complex set of applications with widely differing system resource requirements it may be to your advantage to take control of how the system deals out its resources in order to get the kind of performance you want. You may wish to give more resources to some applications at the expense of other applications. You can do that with commands that work with the allocation of system resources and the structures that control the flow of work through the system. There are tools to help you with this task. These tools can be used to record and report the usage of system resources in your actual working environment. You can use that information to reallocate resources, then use the tools again to see how they affected the overall running of the applications.

A thorough understanding of work management concepts is essential in order to tune the AS/400 to manage a complex set of applications effectively. Knowledge of work management is also important for a clear understanding of what is involved in setting realistic and attainable performance objectives.

OVERVIEW OF WORK MANAGEMENT STRUCTURE AND CONTROL

One method of studying the way the AS/400 controls the flow of work through the system is to observe the resource constraints associated with each job. Because a system is a collection of jobs, we can relate the resource usage of individual jobs to the total collection of jobs that are active at any one time.

Resource constraints are expressed as job attributes. Each job that enters the system, whether an interactive job or a batch job, enters through an environment called a subsystem that routes the job to run in a specific allocation of main storage. That allocation of main storage is called a main storage pool and is identified to the system by a system pool number. Individual jobs do not ordinarily get exclusive use of a main storage pool, although the system can be configured to allow that to happen. In most cases the main storage pool is shared by a subset of other jobs that run on the system. The amount of storage needed in a pool is not necessarily related to the size of the programs that run in the pool.

The "single level store" architecture of the AS/400 lets each program "think" it has access to 281 trillion bytes (2**48) of storage and handles the paging of main memory in and out of the pool without the user needing to be concerned about that process unless the rate of paging becomes excessive. The real concern is not the size of the program, but how many pages are actually being used and the rate at which execution passes from one page to another. For the moment, put aside concerns about how large the pool must be and focus on the process of allocating storage pools.

Storage Pools

Main storage is always divided into pools that restrict activity to a subset of main storage resource. When the system is first powered up, a "machine pool" allocation is reserved for system and operating system usage. This pool is protected from use by user programs, and the remaining main storage may be divided into additional storage pools.

The main storage pool assigned to the job is one of the important job attributes associated with the job. The main storage pool attribute serves two important functions: The first is that it provides a memory resource in which the job can function, and the second is related to the combination of other tasks concurrently running on the system. The ability to run other tasks in other main storage pools means that the job is protected from other jobs that might otherwise encroach upon the memory needed by the first job. This separation of shared main storage resources is important when multiple jobs having very different operating characteristics are running on the system at the same time.

For an example of two jobs with different operating characteristics, consider an interactive order-entry program running while a large program is being compiled. The characteristics of the two jobs are quite different. The compiler tends to use large blocks of main storage to develop tables and references while using relatively large blocks of processing time to perform the compilation. The order-entry job, on the other hand, runs in short bursts. The order-entry operator enters information on the display panel and presses a key that runs a short burst of processing, which results in another display panel of information. The order-entry job spends far more time waiting for operator action than it spends processing the operator's actions. This wait time is commonly referred to as key/think time. The importance of providing separate allocations of main storage for these two types of jobs becomes apparent when one considers what would happen without this separation in a single level store architecture where programs can allocate as much storage as they can use to perform their functions. The compile function would "steal" the inactive pages of main storage used by the order-entry job while the job is waiting at key/think time. By the time the operator presses the Enter key or any other key that gets the attention of the central processing unit, chances are that few if any of the pages of memory it needs will still be in main storage. Remember that the AS/400 architecture uses separate processors to handle input/output functions. Thus the processor does not see the normal data keystrokes and the job remains in a wait state during key/think time. The workstation controller reads all of the workstation keystrokes, controls the placement of keyed data on the screen, and passes only a few of the keystrokes to the central processing unit. The keystrokes that are passed to the CPU are called "function and attention" keys such as the Enter key, function keys, roll or paging keys, etc. When one of these function or attention keys is pressed, key/think time ends and the system must restore pages from auxiliary storage (disk) to main memory if those pages are needed and were stolen by some other task during key/think time. The ensuing delay has an impact on interactive response time.

The AS/400 allows the user to manage this main storage allocation conflict using a construct called main storage pools. Jobs are restricted to drawing needed main storage resources from a designated main storage pool. The job attribute that reflects this storage allocation is the pool ID number, which refers specifically to the pool number in the subsystem description that routed the job to the system.

Subsystems

A new term, subsystem, has been introduced which requires an explanation. All jobs enter the system through a subsystem environment. In order to establish this environment, a subsystem is started using the STRSBS command, which refers to a subsystem description object that describes the environment. The environment provides an entry point for jobs and provides a means of allocating resources to the job. The first of these resource allocations considered here is the allocation of main storage pools.

When the system is first turned on (IMPLed), only two main storage pools are allocated. Pool number 1 is the machine pool, and it is a special allocation of main storage reserved for the operating system. Its size is determined by a system value named QMCHPOOL. All remaining main storage is allocated to pool number 2 named *BASE. Figure 9.1 represents the allocation of main storage after the system has been turned on and before any subsystems have been started. It is possible to run all user jobs in *BASE. As described in the earlier scenario, it is often advantageous to establish additional main storage pools. These pools are defined in subsystem descriptions, and the allocation takes place when subsystems are started. Typically, all subsystems are started when the system is turned on. Subsystems can be started or ended at any time, however, and sometimes this is done to adjust to work load changes throughout a day or week.

As the subsystems are started and the system recognizes the pools defined by the subsystem descriptions, storage allocations are subtracted from *BASE and given to the newly defined pools. The additional storage pools may be private pools that are available only to the subsystem that allocated them, or they may be shared pools, in which case the pool's resources may be shared between two or more subsystems. *BASE is an example of a shared pool that may be shared between multiple subsystems, but there are other shared pools as well. The following scenario follows the process of allocating private pools as three subsystems, A, B, and C, are started in that sequence.

Figure 9.2 represents the status of main storage and its division into pools at the conclusion of the process. The process begins when subsystem A is started via the STRSBS command. Pool ID number 1 within subsystem A is defined as a private pool of size 40, meaning 40K of storage. The subsystem monitor

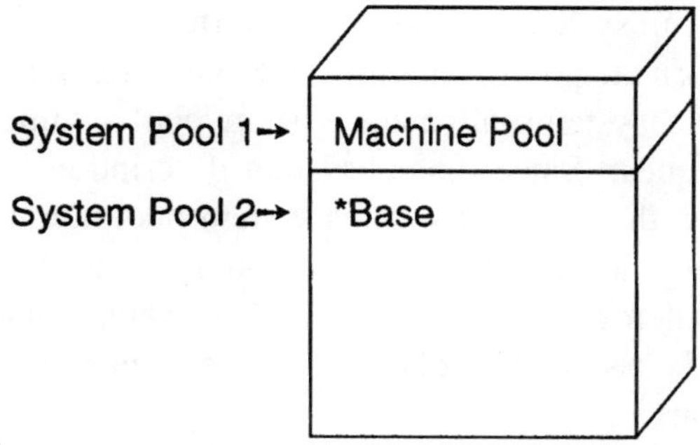

Figure 9.1 Allocation of main storage

program establishes a new system pool of 40K in size. The 40K is subtracted from the size of *BASE. This new pool is given a system pool number of 3. Note that it is pool number 1 in reference to the subsystem description, but it is the third pool known to the system.

Subsystem B is started next. The first pool in subsystem B is known to the subsystem description as pool ID 1, and it specifies that the pool resource used is *BASE. Since *BASE already exists and is a shared pool, no further division of main storage is needed. Jobs routed through subsystem B that are assigned to run in this pool will use the pool resources of *BASE. Subsystem B defines a second pool, pool ID 2, that calls for 1500K of storage in a private pool. System pool number 4 is consequently established at a size of 1500K and that storage is again subtracted from the storage allocated to *BASE. Thus the subsystem pool ID number 2 for subsystem B becomes system pool number 4.

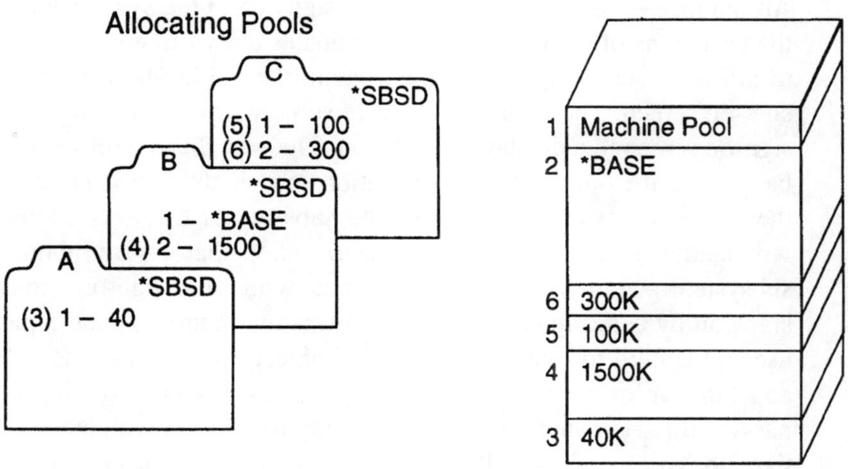

Figure 9.2 Division of main storage into pools

One more subsystem remains to be started—the subsystem named C, which defines two private pools. The first pool in the subsystem calls for a private pool of 100K. The systems allocates system pool number 5 in response to this allocation request. Since the subsystem description calls for a second private pool of 300K, the system allocates system pool number 6 in that amount. The system has now allocated four private pools numbered 3 through 6 in response to the subsystems that were started. You should note that the system pool number that is assigned is related to the sequence in which these three subsystems were started.

Starting these three subsystems in a different sequence would give different system pool numbers to the respective pools. For example, if subsystem C had been the first subsystem started after starting the system, then system pool number 3 would be a 100K private pool and system pool number 4 would be a 300K private pool.

The scenario that has been described shows how main memory resources can be divided into multiple pools. Jobs that run on the system are assigned to draw memory resources from one of the available pools. The way in which this assignment is handled is determined by information in a subsystem that routes the job to its resources. We have just seen how subsystem descriptions determine the division of main memory into pools of memory resources; now we will look at how the subsystem routes jobs to use memory pools and other resources.

Job Routing

We begin looking at the routing of jobs by considering an interactive job first. An interactive job begins when a user signs on to the system and it ends when the user signs off or when the job terminates due to an error condition. In order to allow a user to sign on to the system, the workstation must first display a sign-on screen. The system must have some way of "knowing" how to write a sign-on screen to a display workstation. The way the system knows to do this is based on something called a workstation entry in the subsystem description. For the moment, assume that one of the subsystems that was started contains a workstation entry that names the workstation that we are about to use. The subsystem acquires the workstation and writes the sign-on screen. The user signs on by entering two items of information, a user ID and a password. The user ID is used to find a "user profile" object that contains the valid password and other information associated with the user who is signing on. After the password is validated, the system is ready to proceed with starting the interactive job. The process is called "routing." The workstation entry in the subsystem

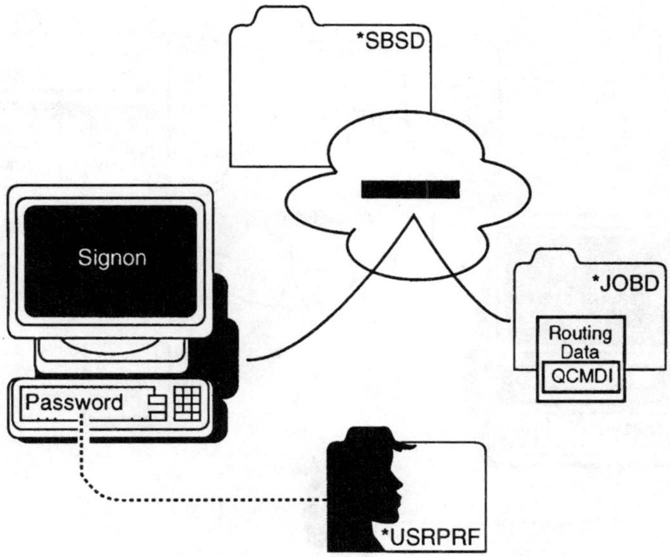

Figure 9.3 AS/400 work management workstation entries

description contains not only the name of the workstation (or some reference that identifies it along with other workstations), it also names a job description object that contains information needed to route the job when the user signs on. Within the job description is a string of characters called routing data. In Figure 9.3 you notice that the routing data in the example consists of five characters, QCMDI. The character string, QCMDI, is then compared to "compare values" in a routing table in the subsystem description where the system looks for a match between the routing data and the compare values in the routing table. See Figure 9.4 for an example of a routing table. In this example there are four table entries. The four compare values are "QCMDI," "QCMDB," "ZEBRA," and "*ANY." In this example, the routing data "QCMDI" from the job description matches with the first compare value in the routing table, so the first entry in the table is used to continue the process of routing this job. Notice that the other values in this table entry are a program name, a class name, and pool ID number one. The pool ID number refers to the pool number in the subsystem description, not the system pool number. Since the system keeps track of which system pool number is associated with each subsystem pool number, it is able to assign the job to the appropriate system pool. In doing so, the job has acquired the attribute that determines the main storage resource that the job can use to do its work. The program name in the table entry is the program that begins to run as the first program for this job. In this case the name of that program is QCMD.

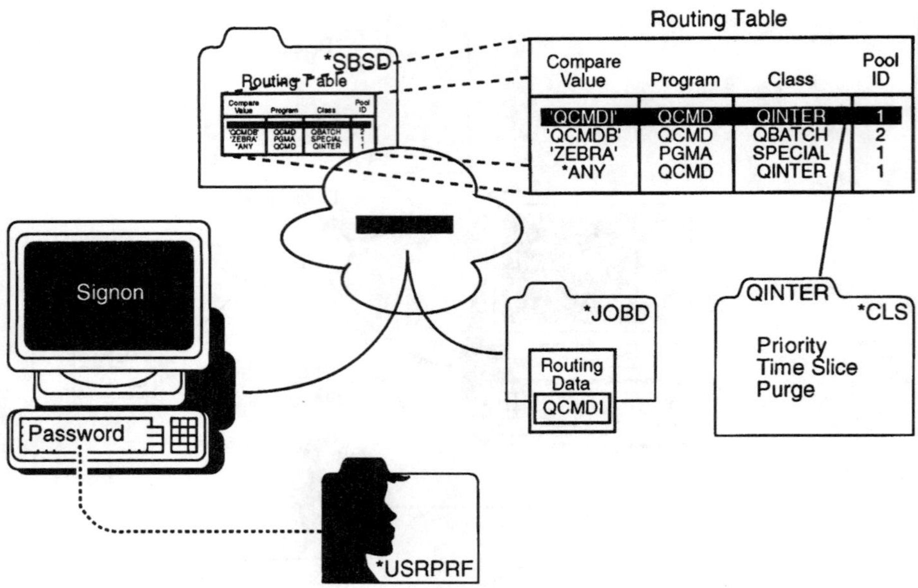

Figure 9.4 AS/400 work management routing

QCMD is the command processing program that interprets and runs commands. When it is the first program initiated in the job routing process, it also performs some special functions that will be addressed later. Figure 9.5 shows one other table item, a class name. This is the name of a "class" object that contains several additional attributes that are assigned to the job and includes "run priority" and "time slice." The job is now ready to run and has been assigned an allocation of main storage resource, a run priority to control how the job will compete with other jobs for processor cycles, and a time slice constraint that specifies the maximum amount of processor time the job is allowed to use before the job must yield the processor to another job.

The simplified description of the process for starting a job given above leaves out a lot of detail that involves the assignment of many other job attributes associated with a job. What is important to notice, however, is the interaction of several objects in the process of routing the job. Those objects are the subsystem description (with its workstation entries, pool IDs, and routing table), a user profile, a job description, and a class. A number of other job attributes that were not discussed in the previous example are drawn from each of these four objects. In addition, the objects can be combined in different ways. For example, the name of the job description can be provided by the user profile instead of by the workstation entry. The point to remember is that these four objects are needed in order to complete the routing of a job.

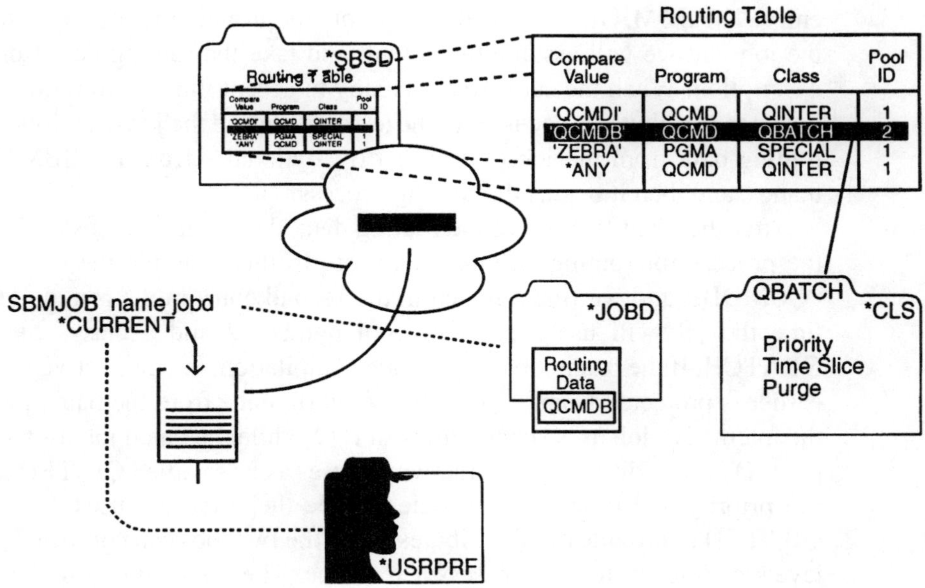

Figure 9.5 Program QCMD

Starting a Batch Job

The next example illustrates how a batch job is started. A batch job does not use a workstation; consequently another type of work entry, a job queue entry, is used. Jobs that run as batch jobs are initially placed in a job queue so that the appropriate subsystem can draw the jobs from the queue as resources in the subsystem become available to run the batch jobs. Consequently, a work entry called a job queue entry must be associated with a subsystem to allow batch jobs to enter the subsystem. The job queue entry serves the same function as a workstation entry, except that the job queue entry is used as an entry point for batch jobs while the workstation entry is used as an entry point for interactive jobs.

Batch jobs are added to a job queue via the SBMJOB (submit job) command. The SBMJOB command references a job queue into which the job is placed. A subsystem has a job queue entry that names the job queue and causes the job to enter through the job queue entry. For this purpose we assume that the interactive user submitted a job for execution in batch via the SBMJOB command. In this case, the user is already known to the system, so the default user profile (*CURRENT) is used to retrieve the attributes provided by the user profile of the user who submitted the job. The name of the job description is provided as a parameter in the submit job command rather than being associated with the work entry. The SBMJOB command can optionally provide the routing data to route the job, but we will assume the default and take the routing data from the job description. When the subsystem is ready to accept the job from the job queue, it gets the attributes it needs from the user profile and the job description, and the routing data from the job description (or optionally from the SBMJOB command), and then it begins the routing process.

After the identification of the routing data, the routing process is identical to the process for routing an interactive job. In this example the routing data is "QCMDB," and we find a match in the second entry in the routing table. This time the job will use subsystem pool number 2 and a class object named QBATCH. If the batch job is a program compilation, the interactive job initiated earlier is protected from main memory interference from the batch job because the interactive job uses subsystem pool ID 1 while the batch job uses subsystem pool ID 2. In addition, the interactive job uses a class named QINTER to provide run priority and time-slice attributes, while the batch job uses a class named QBATCH to provide these attributes. Thus the two jobs can compete at different levels of priority for the processor resource. The interactive job, for example, would be given a higher priority than the batch job so that it can get its small burst of work done quickly and then enter the key/think wait cycle. The batch job, running at a lower priority, can use the processor cycles during the interactive job's key/think wait cycle to get batch work done.

Job Attributes

The previous discussions have shown that there are many job attributes associated with jobs and that these attributes may come from alternate sources. The table in Figure 9.6 provides additional information related to a few job attributes. Notice that the attributes OUTPTY, ENDSEV, LOG, OUTQ, the library list, and routing data (subsystem pool ID) are ordinarily provided by the job description (JOBD). They may be provided on an override basis from the SBMJOB command, however. The routing entry supplies the job with main memory resource via the subsystem pool ID. Other job attributes such as run priority (RUNPTY) and time slice (TIMESLICE) are provided by a class object (CLASS).

If we ignore for the moment the fact that many of the attributes can optionally be provided to batch jobs via the SBMJOB command, we can say that jobs acquire their attributes from the following key sources:

1. Job description
2. Subsystem description with its routing table

3. Class
4. User profile

Our discussion up to this point has made only passing reference to the role that the user profile plays in starting jobs. The password is associated with the user profile and serves to prevent unauthorized access to the system. The profile does more than that, however. It also provides some of the attributes used by the job and participates in determining which programs begin to run when the job is initiated.

Look at the routing table once more in Figure 9.5 and notice that QCMD is named as the program that will begin to run when the job starts. QCMD is the program that presents the command entry screen and interprets commands that are entered on that screen or on any screen that presents a command entry line. QCMD performs an important additional function when it is the program initiated via the routing entry. When QCMD is initiated from the routing entry for an interactive job, it checks the user profile for an initial program associated with the profile. If it finds one listed in the user profile, it calls and begins executing it. If it does not find one, it checks for an initial menu in the user profile. If it finds this, then that menu is presented to the interactive user. If

AS/400 Work Management

SBMJOB	SBSD	RTGE	JOBD	CLASS	Sources of Job Attributes
*	X		*		Subsystem Name
X			X		OUTPTY
			X		ENDSEV
X			X		LOG
X			X		OUTQ
X			X		Library List
*	*	X	*		Subsystem pool id
		*		X	RUNPTY
		*		X	TIMESLICE
		*		X	CPUTIME
		*		X	MAXTMPSTG
					...etc...

* Dependency

Figure 9.6 Job attributes

QCMD fails to find either an initial program or an initial menu, then it presents the command entry screen to the user.

QCMD performs a different function when it is initiated for a batch job. The SBMJOB command passes a command that is to be executed as a character string. This string is referred to as the "request data" (RQSDTA). These are examples of SBMJOB commands:

```
SBMJOB CMD(CALL PROGB) JOB(MYBATCHJOB)
```

or

```
SBMJOB JOB(MYBATCHJOB) RQSDTA('CALL PROGB')
```

Both commands do the same thing, because the CMD value in the first example is treated as "request data." QCMD checks the request data associated with the SBMJOB and executes that command. Thus a SBMJOB command that intends to run PROGB in a batch job would include the CALL PROGB command as the request data or the command. When the job is initiated, PROGB will execute in the batch job.

This overview of work management structure and control provides a first look at some of the important resources that are available on the AS/400 to get work accomplished. In addition the controls for managing these resources have been identified in the form of four objects, user profiles, job descriptions, subsystem descriptions, and classes. An administrator of AS/400 resources can use these four objects to control how work enters the system and how the system resources are applied to getting the work done.

WORKING WITH WORK MANAGEMENT OBJECTS

Objects that contribute job attributes to jobs were identified in the previous sections. A closer look at some of these objects reveals controls that operate across multiple jobs to control the number of jobs that compete concurrently for system resources. The term used to denote a restriction of this type is "activity level." Activity level restrictions are applied at the total system level to control the number of active jobs that are allowed to share the processor usage at any one time via a system value, QMAXACTLVL. The QMAXACTLVL does not limit the number of jobs that may be initiated at the same time; it only limits a subset of initiated jobs that can concurrently share the processor. The limit to the number of jobs that may be initiated is controlled at several other points. Subsystems can restrict the number of jobs that are allowed to use the resources of a main storage pool concurrently by means of a maximum activity level associated with the pool. At an even more detailed level, the routing entry within a subsystem specifies the maximum number of routing steps (jobs) that can be active at the same time through this routing entry.

Backing up one more step to the work entries in a subsystem, each work entry (workstation entry, job queue entry, etc.) specifies a maximum number of jobs that can be active at the same time from the work entry. The granular activity controls provide a great deal of flexibility for controlling the amount of work the system is allowed to process at a given point in time. The reason for all these controls is to avoid giving the system so much work to do at the same time that it spends an inordinate part of its processing time trying to manage multiple tasks instead of doing the work of a more limited set of tasks. When a system spends too much of its time trying to manage a large number of tasks, we say that the system is "thrashing." This should be avoided because a thrashing system does less work that is of value to the users. Activity levels are the controls that limit the number of jobs that run at the same time.

QMAXACTLVL, the system value, is different from the other activity level controls. All of the other activity level controls limit the number of jobs that may enter the system and run at the same time. QMAXACTLVL, on the other hand, limits the number of those jobs that may occupy the active state. All jobs in the system occupy one of three states—active, wait, or ineligible. Figure 9.7 illustrates the relationships between the total number of jobs, the number of active jobs, and the number of jobs in the active state. The active jobs are those that exist in main storage and process work requests by the application. Jobs in the wait state are waiting because a needed resource is not available. A program

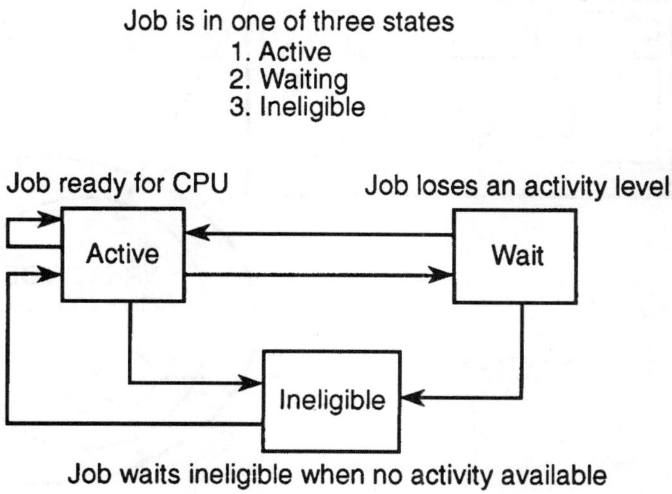

Figure 9.7 Accommodating the hardware job state transitions

may be in the wait state because the job is waiting on a workstation. For example, the workstation is in key/think mode, and the operator has not pressed a key that requires the use of central processor resources. The third state, ineligible, is for programs that have work to do, but the maximum number of activities are in use so the system cannot accept more work. See the IBM publication, *AS/400 Programming: Work Management Guide*, SC41-8078, for a detailed description of these three states in the chapter on performance tuning. The AS/400 accounts for jobs that have finished running, but whose output remains in an output queue. Any job whose output has not been disposed of is counted among the total jobs in the system. Thus the total number of jobs usually is larger than the number of jobs that may be active at the same time.

Figure 9.8 shows the relationships between the jobs in the system and lists the AS/400 commands that display job statistics. The WKRSYSSTS (work with system status) command lists the total number of jobs in the system. WRKACTJOB (work with active jobs) displays the number of active jobs and also shows some performance data and status information related to each job. The number of jobs in the active state is a variable that changes rapidly depending on how much work the system is doing. The performance measurement tools can collect data and report the number of jobs in the active state at various points in time. Performance measurement topics, however, are outside the scope of this book. The maximum number of jobs allowed in the active state is controlled by the QMAXACTLVL system value and can be viewed via the DSPSYSVAL (display system values) command.

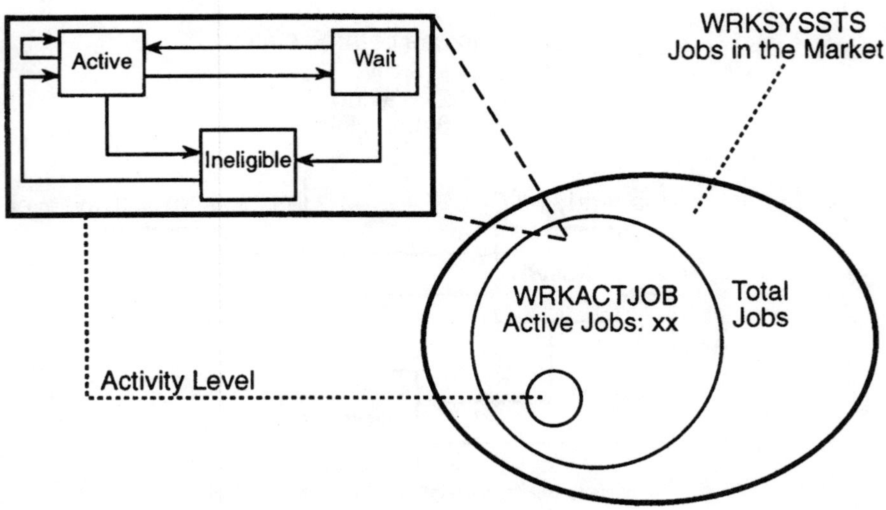

Figure 9.8 AS/400 work management jobs and system activity

Control Points

The foregoing information provides a background for understanding how the activity in the system is controlled. The next step is to identify the objects that specify these control points. For starters, it should be noted that the only control that is not associated with a system object is the system value QMAXACTLVL.

The first point where activity controls may be applied is job entry points. These are represented by the work entries within subsystem descriptions. Each entry point may restrict the number of jobs that may concurrently be active as a result of entering through the work entry. A value is not required, however, because one of the options is the special value, *NOMAX, instead of a number. The system employs other means of restricting activity when *NOMAX is used. The *NOMAX special value is commonly associated with workstation entries. It usually makes sense to use it this way because the number of workstations attached to a system is limited, and ordinarily the system is expected to allow any or all workstations to sign on and perform work. Job queue entries, on the other hand, are frequently added to subsystems with a restriction on the maximum active jobs. The default value for the ADDJOBQE command is MAXACT(1). Note that the maximum activity is specified in the subsystem description when the job queue is added. It is not directly associated with the job queue itself. Consequently, the CRTJOBQ (create job queue) command does not make provision for an activity level, and the ADDJOBQE command provides the means of controlling the activity level.

Commands that add work entries to subsystem descriptions with MAXACT parameters include the following:

ADDWSE
ADDJOBQE
ADDCMNE
ADDAJE
ADDPJE
ADDAJE

The MAXACT values can be changed with the CHGxxx commands that correspond to the ADDxxx commands. Routing entries within subsystem descriptions also provide a means for limiting the number of jobs the routing entry can route at the same time. The ADDRTGE command does this via the MAXACT parameter.

When subsystem descriptions are created, one or more storage pools are associated with the subsystem description. Storage pools also limit the number of jobs that can run at the same time in the pool. This is specified for private pools when a subsystem is created via the POOL parameter with the CRTSBSD (create subsystem description) command or when it is changed via the CHGSBSD command. A MAXJOBS parameter in those same commands places a limit on the number of jobs that may be active at the same time in the subsystem controlled by the subsystem description. Shared pools, like private pools, have a MAXACT parameter associated with each one. The attributes associated with shared pools are not specified in the subsystem description objects because the shared pools can be shared across multiple subsystem descriptions.

Consequently another command, WRKSHRPOOL (work with shared pools) is used to adjust the maximum active value and also the size of the shared pool. Even though there are many control points for limiting the number of jobs that may be active at the same time, the process for determining whether the limit has been reached is not complicated. A description of the sequence for starting jobs based on activity limits follows:

1. The job will start if the limit associated with the work entry will support another job. Go to the next step.
2. The job begins the routing process. It will fail if the routing step cannot support another job based on the routing step limit. If the job can be supported by the limit, go to the next step.
3. The routing step identifies the pool that provides the memory resource for the job. If the job limit associated with the pool cannot support another job at this time, the job fails. Otherwise go to the next step.
4. The subsystem description MAXJOBS value is checked to determine whether another job can be supported by the subsystem. If not, the job fails. Otherwise the job completes the routing steps and the job starts (becomes an active job.)

After a job becomes active, it moves between the three states (active, wait, ineligible) described earlier. Active jobs compete for processor resources, memory resources, and other system resources based on run priority, time slice, memory pool, and the devices associated with each job. Up to this point, the process of routing a job and providing its job attributes has been described in the "Overview of Work Management Structure and Control" section, and the means for restricting the number of jobs that can run at the same time has been described in this section, "Working with Work Management Objects." The commands and objects that control the attributes and activity levels have also been described.

Another concept that has been introduced but not described in detail is priority. Priority scheduling is the means the system uses to choose work from a queue of potential activity. Run priority, for example, determines what preference will be given to jobs that are competing for processor resources. It was noted earlier that active jobs exist in one of three states at any point in time—active, wait, or ineligible. This implies that in a busy system, the active jobs are somehow queued in each of these states, because the processor can process only one job at a time. The AS/400 uses prioritized queues to handle the scheduling of activity. Some of these queues are created and/or controlled by the user and some of them are reserved for the exclusive use of the system. The description that follows begins with job queues and ends by describing queues used exclusively by the system.

Job Queues

Figure 9.9 is an illustration of a prioritized queue. As items (jobs) are placed in a job queue, they are arranged in a first-in-first-out (FIFO) sequence within job priority on the job queue. The illustration shows items as lines of three weights. The heaviest lines represent the jobs with the highest priority in the queue, while the lightest lines represent the jobs having the lowest priority. In this illustration, jobs enter at the top of the queue and are scheduled (withdrawn) from the bottom of the queue.

Suppose the jobs in the illustration are at priorities of 10, 20, and 50. Just as priority 1 is usually associated with the highest priority, the lowest numbers are given the highest priority on the AS/400. Thus priority 10 jobs are represented by the entries at the bottom of the queue and will be the first to be scheduled as the system makes resources available for new jobs from this queue. Likewise, the jobs with a job priority on the job queue of 50 are represented by the light lines at the top of the queue. It should be noted that job priority on the job queue

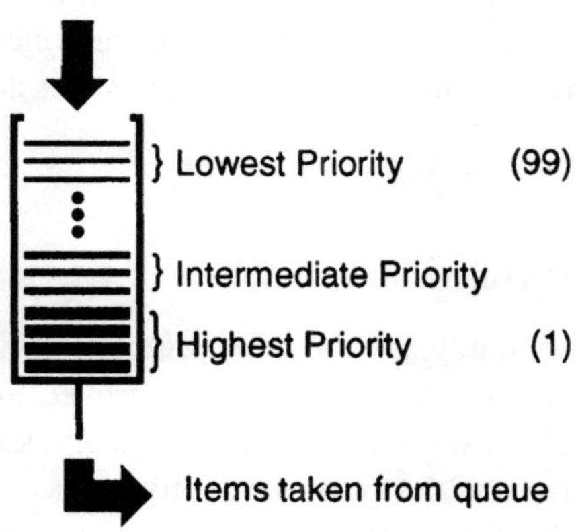

Figure 9.9 AS/400 work managment prioritized queues

is a different priority from run priority. Job priority on the job queue controls the sequence in which jobs are scheduled from the job queue, while run priority determines how the job will compete for the processor resources after the job has been scheduled as active. The concept of the prioritized queue as described here is a concept that applies to other types of queues.

System Queues

Return to Figure 9.8, which illustrates the three possible states of active jobs. Since the AS/400 is a multitasking system, it is possible to have a collection of jobs existing in each of the three states. The system uses prioritized queues to manage the transfer of jobs from one state to another. These queues are used exclusively by the system, so the user does not have direct access to them. The user exercises indirect control by assigning run priorities and time-slice values to jobs via class objects and the other controls described earlier that determine the way a job is routed through a subsystem. As jobs in the active state wait for resources, they may move to the wait state. If they exceed the limits of processor usage determined by the time-slice value and if other jobs need the resources of the processor, they are moved to the ineligible state. Within each of these states, they occupy a position in a prioritized queue associated with the state.

Jobs that are in the active state, for example, must share processor resources. The system has a preset time (not controlled by the user) that it will allot to each job in the active state. Assuming the value is 50 milliseconds, then the system will give each active job up to 50 milliseconds of processor time before switching the resource to another job on the active state queue. In this way jobs in the active state share processor resources among them. The maximum number of jobs that may exist in the active state at any one time is set by the system value QMAXACTLVL. The IBM manual, *AS/400 Programming: Work Management Guide*, SC41-8078, has a chapter on performance tuning, with a section on job states that provides more detail about job states and transitions from one state to another.

Tuning to Improve Performance

The first step in tuning a system for better performance is to determine what part of the system activity needs to be improved and under what conditions the improvement is desired. In a complex system, the tuning needs often vary with the time of day and the type of activity in the system. Accordingly, it is often possible to identify several times when the system needs to be tuned and the requirements at each of these times are probably different. The *AS/400 Pro-*

gramming: Work Management Guide suggests how to gather information about performance using standard system commands. One way to begin the process is to identify the critical time period when performance needs the most attention. Gather the information while the system is operating under a peak load during that time frame.

Always keep a record of the performance values that are in effect before making changes. Sometimes attempts to change an environment end up making things worse rather than better, so it is better to proceed without burning bridges that may prove valuable during a retreat. The information should include which subsystems are operating, the system pool sizes, routing table entries in each subsystem, values in each of the class objects, job description values, etc.

Before making a change to any value, ensure that it is backed up and adequately documented. The handiest method for restoring the starting values is to write a CLP (Control Language program) that restores values to what existed before beginning the tuning process. This provides a method of rapid retreat.

Follow the suggestions in the manual that are under the topic of basic tuning. Before making any changes, set the system value of QPFRADJ to 0 to turn off automatic performance adjustments. If it is not set to zero, the system may try to re-adjust the changes you make. Be sure to make the changes and try them while the system is operating under the type of load that was in effect when the performance data was collected. Otherwise, any changes made are relatively meaningless. If these changes resulted in the desired improvement, the commands that set up this environment can be combined into a CLP that quickly establishes the appropriate environment.

Having CLPs that establish performance related values is especially handy if the system operates under multiple applications. Each program can quickly establish the environment that is most suitable for the mix of applications. For example, if a system runs a heavy mix of interactive applications during the normal working hours and the objective is to provide good interactive response time at the expense of batch jobs, then the system can be tuned to meet that objective and a CLP can be written that establishes the appropriate environment. That program might be named TUNEINTER or any other name of your choice. A program named TUNEBATCH might be developed to set the environment that is most appropriate for a heavy batch environment, such as nightly batch update runs. If this theoretical system must also run in an environment that has fewer interactive jobs and where batch performance is important during early morning hours and evening hours, then a TUNEMIXED program might be helpful. As the system environment changes, these tailored programs can quickly set the predetermined values needed to meet performance objectives.

This elementary discussion of performance tuning is intended to point you toward understanding some of the important elements related to resource utilization and its impact on performance. IBM provides a tool, IBM Performance Tools/400, product number 5738-PT1, that gathers performance information. It also includes tools to help you analyze the data it collects. You can also write your own programs to gather specific information about your system or about specific applications on your system. These tools are particularly helpful when trying to improve performance or to squeeze the last ounce (or milliliter) of work out of a large and complex system.

As systems become larger, the task of identifying performance bottlenecks becomes more involved, and tools are essential to make sure that all the bases have been covered. This is true when planning to upgrade a system to handle a larger work load. A cursory analysis of the current workload might point toward needing a larger processor. Other factors related to an increased workload might reveal that solving a compute bottleneck with a faster processor will only result in a new bottleneck such as an insufficient number of disk access mechanisms to handle the increased data volumes. The product includes a modeling tool to help identify bottlenecks, given anticipated increased workloads. The BEST/1 capacity planner in this product identifies processing limits of your system so that the effect of upgrading can be evaluated to include the following:

Processing unit
Main storage
Disk input/output processors
Disk storage controllers and arms
Display stations
Local workstation input/output processors
Remote workstation controllers
Communications input/output processors

The BEST/1 planner can use input from one or a combination of several sources. You can import the workload description collected from the performance monitor and combine it with user workload descriptions. You can also define your performance objectives. These data are analyzed to provide you with a set of recommendations that may include hardware upgrade recommendations with identification of system resources that may become bottlenecks.

SUMMARY

Subsystems provide an entry point and an environment for jobs that run on the AS/400. Two of the several types of work entries are points of entry for interactive jobs (the workstation entry) and for batch jobs (the job queue entry). As jobs enter a subsystem, a job description provides routing data, which is compared to information in a routing table within the subsystem. When a compare value match is found in the table, the associated table entry provides the job with a pool ID, which identifies the main storage resource the job will use, a class name that provides processor resource restrictions, and the name of the program that will begin to run. The attributes for the job are collected from four objects—the user profile, a job description, a subsystem description with its routing table, and a class. A person who is in charge of administering the resources of an AS/400 can use these four object types to control the resources the job is allowed to use to get the work done.

Getting work done on the AS/400 with multiple users and multiple tasks is accomplished by allocating resources of the system to the various tasks it must perform. Each task uses system resources consisting of main memory, computer cycles for computation, disk storage, workstations, and other devices. Restraints on the amount of resources allocated to any given job are defined by objects and commands that use them. A subsystem, defined by a subsystem description object, provides an environment for jobs that run in the system and also serves as the focal point for assigning resources when the job is started through a process called routing. AS/400 has commands that allow resource allocations to be modified so the performance of the system is changed. A system can be "tuned" for performance by manipulating the resources allocated to the jobs that are active in the system. A set of performance tools is available from IBM to aid you in measuring and collecting performance data. That data can then be used by other tools to make recommendations for tuning the system and upgrading the hardware.

10

Future Directions for the AS/400

Now that you have a basic understanding of the AS/400 and how it functions, let us take a look at some future directions for the AS/400. This is important for any AS/400 user, from long established sites to those just installing a new system. As new features and capabilities become available, users must decide which to implement and which to forgo. While many of these decisions may be based on business needs, it is important to keep in mind the direction of the industry in general and the direction of your particular hardware vendor. If the industry (and your specific vendor) change or upgrade hardware and operating systems and you choose not to follow, it may be difficult in the future to find support and applications for less than current versions of the hardware and the operating system.

Imagine if you will trying today to find packaged application software for the CP/M operating system or hardware for an Osborne computer. While these examples may be a bit outrageous, they illustrate the point that generally support and applications are available only for those systems that currently dominate the market. This is not to say that it is necessary to purchase every upgrade, but rather that it is important to keep abreast of developments and how they may affect your system now and in the future. In this chapter we will look at two areas in which developments may impact on the AS/400: Operating systems and communications.

OPERATING SYSTEMS

Since its introduction, the OS/400 operating system has undergone several upgrades and enhancements. The latest version, V2R3, supports increased memory and disk storage in addition to new AS/400 peripherals.[1] While a robust operating system, OS/400 is still proprietary. That is, it runs only on the AS/400 platform. A major trend in the computing industry has been to move towards open systems. Open systems are defined as those that conform to a set of standards and provide access to multiple vendor solutions.[2] What this essentially means is that applications need not be developed for a particular platform or operating system. Applications are portable across systems and any vendors' hardware could be used with any application. In terms of operating systems, this usually means using some variant of the UNIX operating system. This is the type of environment in which the AS/400 must compete in the future.

A recent survey showed that in the overall operating systems market, OS/400 and UNIX each accounted for 19 percent of total market revenue in 1992, but estimated that by 1997 OS/400 would fall to 8 percent while UNIX was projected to grow to 44 percent.[3] While this may seem to predict the demise of OS/400, this operating system still has several major strong points. The large installed base of the AS/400 and the OS/400 operating system would tend to indicate that it is popular with mid-range system users. While the AS/400 is not an open system by definition, the large amount of packaged software available for the AS/400 provides users with a wide range of applications. The OS/400 operating system also provides a "mainframe-like" environment on a mid-range platform. Users appreciate the security and control of the mainframe at the cost of a mid-range system. In an effort to capitalize on the AS/400, IBM is attempting to position the AS/400 as an open server. While the AS/400 itself is not an open platform, it can act as a server for other open systems. Through a number of communications protocols, the AS/400 and its database can provide data to UNIX clients.[4] This also positions the AS/400 for a role as a server in client/server computing applications. In this type of situation, the AS/400 could serve a dual role, that of a traditional mid-range processing platform and that of a database server. Figure 10.1 shows an example for this type of situation.

In Figure 10.1 the AS/400 acts a processing platform for the attached 5250 terminals and PCs. Additionally, applications running on UNIX workstations such as the RS6000 would be accessing data stored on the AS/400. This data sharing could be accomplished by a number of methods such as file transfer and SQL calls.

The OS/400 operating system itself may be upgraded in the future to take advantage of new technologies such as reduced instruction set computing or RISC. Other operating systems such as Microsoft's Windows NT may be ported to the AS/400.[5] Even in light of the predicted growth in UNIX, OS/400 will continue to be a viable operating system and could potentially benefit from the growth in UNIX.

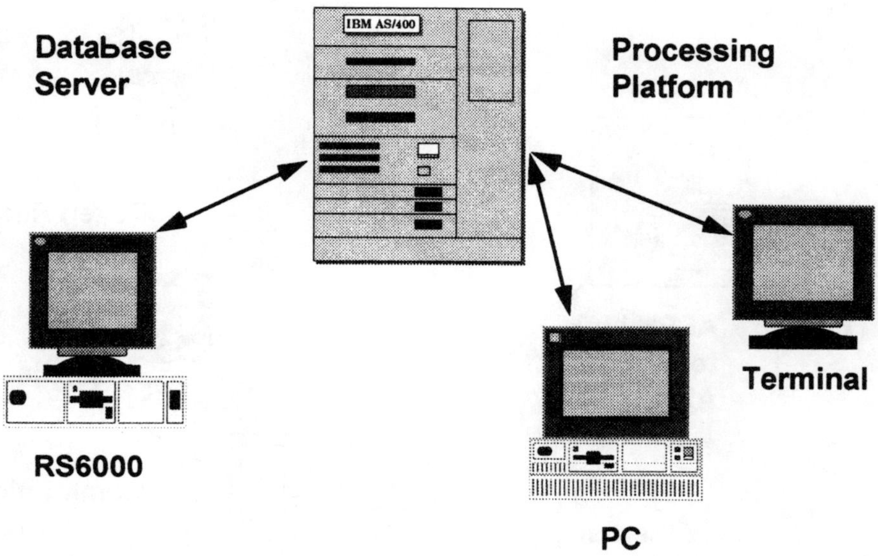

Figure 10.1 The AS/400 as a server

COMMUNICATIONS

In the future, the importance of data communications can be expected to grow. This is true with the AS/400. Initially, the AS/400 was designed to function within an IBM SNA, but as communications between heterogeneous systems become more and more common, the communications capabilities of the AS/400 have expanded to meet these needs. A major development in this area is TCP/IP support for the AS/400. As UNIX has become the open operating system standard, TCP/IP has become the open communications protocol. Heterogenous systems, regardless of operating system, can communicate via the TCP/IP protocol. This communications support is what enables the AS/400 to act as an open database server even with its proprietary operating system. Another advantage of the AS/400 is its ability to communicate with a number of different communications protocols. In addition to TCP/IP, the AS/400 can still communicate in an SNA network via APPN. This is valuable in situations of mixed vendor hardware. Often in an enterprise it is not uncommon to find an IBM mainframe, one or more AS/400s, as well as mid-range open systems. The AS/400 has the capability to communicate to all of these platforms. In terms of workstation connectivity, the AS/400 can communicate with terminals, PCs, UNIX workstations, and even the Macintosh.[6] LAN support for the AS/400 has

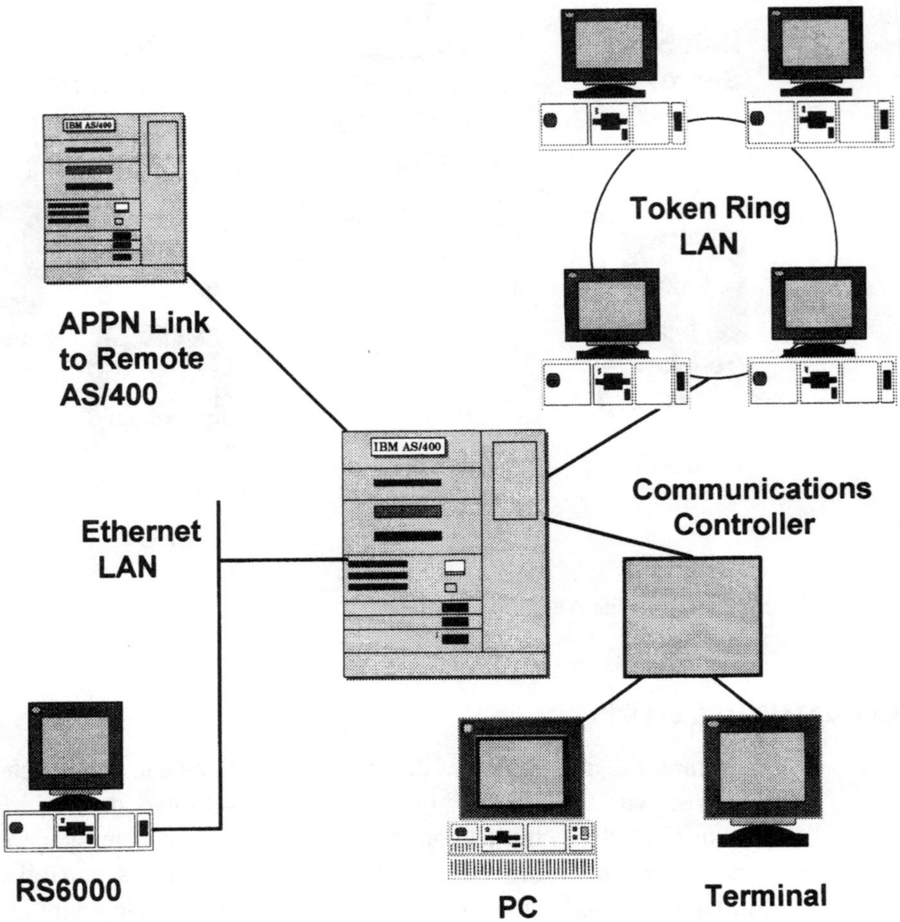

Figure 10.2 AS/400 communications options

been expanded to include the Ethernet as well as token ring topologies. Adapters for high–speed media such as fiber are available for the AS/400. The AS/400 can act as a Netware server for LAN clients.[7] Figure 10.2 illustrates some of the communications options available with the AS/400.

In this type of configuration, the AS/400 is connected to traditional "dumb" terminals via a communications controller. Additionally, PC and Mac users access the AS/400 through terminal emulation. LAN clients access the AS/400 via a token ring network while UNIX clients on an RS6000 workstation access data on the RS6000 through and Ethernet connection. In addition to these clients, the AS/400 is connected to an APPN network and communicates with another connected AS/400. This is just a simple example of the many communications options available with the AS/400.

In general, the AS/400 offers a number of advantages in terms of communications. It can operate in "legacy" SNA environments as well as in open TCP/IP environments. As new transmission protocols such as the asynchronous transmission mode, or ATM evolve, it can be expected that the AS/400 will be able to take advantage of them.

SUMMARY

The AS/400 is one of the most popular mid-range computer systems available. Its continued success and the large third party hardware and software markets attest to this fact. Each year newer, more powerful models are introduced and the product line continues to expand. New roles such as that of database server are being found for the AS/400. The AS/400 definitely has a place in client/server computing and was one of the major factors in the overall trend toward downsizing. While some may feel that UNIX and the RISC-based midrange systems will challenge the AS/400's position in the mid-range market, the AS/400, like its mainframe predecessors, will continue to play a role in the enterprise computing environments of the future.

REFERENCES

1. *IBM AS/400 System Additions*, International Business Machines Corporation, 1993. p. 15.
2. Tom Wheeler, *Open Systems Handbook*, NY: Bantam Books, 1992, p.3 .
3. Alan Radding, "Multiple Server OS Options Leading to Hybrid Shops," *Software*, November 1993, p. 64.
4. "The AS/400: Architecture for the '90s," supplement to *Datamation*, November 1, 1993, p. S-33.
5. Robert Moran, "Deconstructing the AS/400," *Information Week*, August 23, 1993, p. 18.
6. "The AS/400: Architecture for the '90s," op. cit. p. S-33.
7. "The AS/400: Architecture for the '90s," op. cit. p. S-34.

Appendix A

Configuring PC Support for the HP Laserjet

You can use the PFTSETUP program to change the characteristics of the PC Support Printer Sessions. You may need this program if you have a printer on your PC that uses unsupported printer control codes. Additionally, you may want to change the behavior of an existing printer to improve its performance. PFTSETUP is a DOS-based program.

If you are using OS/2 PC Support, you must copy PFTSETUP.COM, PFTA0100.PG1, and PFTA0100.HP1 from the \QIWSFLR\MRI2924 directory on the AS/400 drive to the PC Support directory on your local drive. You should also copy *.PFT (or at least the specific .PFT files you need) from \QIWSFLR to your local drive. Then, run the PFTSETUP program from a DOS window or DOS full screen session.

You will need technical documentation describing your printer codes in order to use the PFTSETUP program. To begin the program, type:

```
PFTSETUP
```

from the PC Support directory. You will be asked whether to Create Table or Revise Table. Choose whichever applies. The following example will revise the HPLASER2.PFT file to better support the HP LaserJet Series II. By following the descriptions, you should be able to apply the equivalent codes for your own printer.

Enter the name of the printer function table (HPLASER2.PFT for this example), the printer port for testing the table (1 for LPT1, 2 for LPT2, etc.), and whether the printer uses continuous (C) or cut paper (P). Continuous paper is sufficient for most applications, even if the printer handles cut forms.

A menu of printer functions appears. These functions include Initialization and Reset, Vertical/Horizontal Spacing, Highlighting, Paper/Page Options, Typestyles/Character Sets, and User-defined Controls. A final selection, Function Selection Tests, must be run after the codes have been defined. This validates the table so that it can be used by PC Support.

INITIALIZATION AND RESET

Begin with initialization and reset. You may enter two codes here: The Start of Document Initialization and the End of Document Reset. All PFT code sequences use hexidecimal coding. A LaserJet printer uses Esc E to reset the printer. In hexidecimal, the Esc character is 1B and capital "E" is 45. So, you would enter **1B 45** to select Esc E. Normally, this escape sequence would apply to both the start of document and end of document. This guarantees that the printer will start from a known state (default settings) and will return to a default state after PC Support is done printing so the next application that uses the printer does not get the wrong font (e.g., compressed or landscape printing).

Sending control codes at the end of a print job can cause problems. If the printer is on a network (or uses a print spooler), the extra codes after the final page may cause a blank page to print at the end of every job. Since most applications send a reset before printing begins, it is sometimes preferable to leave the End of Document Reset blank. A third parameter on the Initialization and Reset page specifies a file, called a Control Sequence File, that has a list of reset or page setup commands. Normally, this entry should remain blank.

VERTICAL/HORIZONTAL SPACING

The next menu selection sets vertical and horizontal line spacing. It leads to another menu that includes a number of important options for configuring the printer.

The first option is Lines per Inch (lpi). This menu selects the codes that set 6 lpi and 8 lpi printing (the two most common options). On the LaserJet, 6 lpi is **1B 26 6C 36 44** (Esc &l6D) and 8 lpi is **1B 26 6C 38 44** (Esc &l8D).

If you like, you can test the setting by pressing F5. The printer will first print a page that says, "Printed Output." PFTSETUP will ask whether this actually printed (if you have a spooler or network printer, it may not). If you are on a network or using a spooler, then answer "N." This will force the print job to close and the page to print, and then you can continue with the test. This also tells PFTSETUP how to handle your printer. The F5 option is available from other code entry screens, too.

The next menu sets variable line spacing. Some printers (such as the LaserJet) can set a wide range of line spacing attributes by using a formula. If your printer allows only fixed line spacing settings, you can skip this selection. Otherwise, enter the line spacing codes substituting the letter "n" for the variable that sets the spacing size. For the LaserJet, this is **1B 26 6C n 43**. You may also enter the maximum value for n (**126**), the offset (**-0**), and the size of the increment in inches (**1 / 48**). Some printers use an offset so that a null character need not be sent to the printer if 0 line spacing is selected. For example, 0 line spacing would use a value of 1. On such a printer, -1 would be entered for the offset.

Indexing functions move the paper (or cursor on a page printer) forward or backward. This allows for special formatting such as superscripts and subscripts (note that not all of the functions are enabled by PC Support, but completing the entire table may leave you with a more robust driver if PC Support is later enhanced). The LaserJet uses the following codes:

Begin Superscript **1B 2A 70 2D 32 30 59**
End Superscript **1B 2A 70 2B 32 30 59**
Begin Superscript **1B 2A 70 2B 32 30 59**
End Superscript **1B 2A 70 2D 32 30 59**
1/2 Index Up (Reverse) **1B 2A 70 2D 32 35 59**
1/2 Index Down (Forward) **1B 2A 70 2B 32 35 59**
Reverse Index **1B 26 61 2D 31 52**

The next menu, Pitches, defines six different type size settings. The most important are the 10, 12, and either 15 or 17.1. Of these, the LaserJet has 16.66 available (although the scalable fonts of the LaserJet Series III can handle any size), so you must choose between 15 or 17.1 or set both to the same codes. Some sizes may not be available on your laser printer; in this case, the printer will select the closest matching size.

Set 5 Pitch: **1B 28 73 35 48**
Set 8.55 Pitch: **1B 28 73 38 2E 35 35 48**
Set 10 Pitch: **1B 26 6B 30 53**
Set 12 Pitch: **1B 26 6B 34 53**
Set 15 Pitch: **1B 26 6B 32 53** (actually 16.66)
Set 17.1 Pitch: **1B 26 6B 32 53** (actually 16.66)

The horizontal motion index tells the printer how to override the current character width spacing. Thus, for example, you can tell the printer to squeeze a 10 pitch typeface into a 12 pitch spacing. The settings are similar to the variable line spacing set earlier (using n as a variable for the actual number). For the

LaserJet, the control sequence is **1B 26 6B n 48**. The maximum is **255**, the offset is **-0**, and the increment in inches is **1/120**.

Horizontal relative movement specifies the code to move the printhead (or cursor) to an arbitrary horizontal position, relative to the current position (e.g., move 3 inches right, or 2 inches left). For forward relative movement, the LaserJet codes are **1B 26 61 2B n 48**, the maximum is **999**, the offset is **-0**, and the increment in inches is **1/720**. For backward relative movement, the codes are **1B 26 61 2D n 48**, the maximum is **999**, the offset is **-0**, and the increment in inches is **1/720**.

HIGHLIGHTING

Highlighting sets the codes for boldface, underlining, and near-letter quality printing. The latter generally applies to dot matrix printers that have separate draft and NLQ modes.

Begin Emphasis (Bold): **1B 28 73 33 42**
End Emphasis (Bold): **1B 28 73 30 42**
Begin Underline: **1B 26 64 30 44**
End Underline: **1B 26 64 40**
Begin NLQ: [leave blank]
End NLQ: [leave blank]

PAPER/PAGE OPTIONS

These are some of the most important settings for ensuring smooth operation of your printer. At the time of this printing, the PC Support LaserJet drivers always inserted a manual feed select code when the AS/400 sent output to the printer. This had the very disconcerting effect of forcing the user to either feed the pages manually or hit the Continue button on the printer to ignore the feed selection.

These codes are defined in the Paper Handling screen. Although there are a number of options here, you should probably limit the definitions to the tray selection codes (and set Collate to **F**). Leave the other codes blank:

Bottom Tray Select and Feed: **1B 26 6C 34 48 1B 26 6C 30 4F**
Top Tray Select and Feed: **1B 26 6C 31 48 1B 26 6C 30 4F**
Envelope Tray Select and Feed: **1B 26 6C 36 48 1B 26 6C 31 4F**

Paper positioning designates the location of the printhead (or cursor) for the start of each new page relative to the upper left corner of the page. Many dot matrix printers can cover the entire page area and should be set to 0. But page printers (such as laser printers) and printers with automatic sheet feeders frequently have an unprintable area on the page. For a LaserJet Series II, the distance from the top paper edge should be **60/300**, the distance from the left paper edge should be **50/300**, and the location should be **R** (distances are measured right from the edge of the paper). For a laser printer, these settings apply to all three paper handling functions: continuous forms, manual feed, and automatic feed.

Page length codes can be set for either lines or inches. The LaserJet measures page length in lines. The control sequence for set page length (lines) is **1B 26 6C n 50** with a maximum value of **999** and and offset of **-0**.

The left margin settings can be ignored, since they have little bearing on data processing output. Likewise, carrier return/line feed need not be set unless your printer uses unusual codes for terminating a line (very unlikely).

Two settings, multiple copies and landscape paper handling, apply only to page printers. You will not need multiple copy support, and you can safely ignore it. Landscape paper handling is not currently supported, but if you want to add the codes, you can simply copy the paper handling values, substituting **31** instead of **30** for the second to last value. For example, the top tray select code is **1B 26 6C 31 48 1B 26 6C 30 4F**, and the top tray landscape code is **1B 26 6C 31 48 1B 26 6C 31 4F**.

Setting the type styles and user-defined controls are beyond the scope of this book. Suffice it to say that you may want to change the type styles settings if you have special character set needs. Examples would include foreign language support, special symbol support, or character-based graphics emulation of the PC extended graphics characters (which allow simple line-drawing and shading).

After you have defined all of the control codes, you must run the function selection tests. You should select Run All Printer Tests, but be forewarned that these tests take some time and will use a lot of paper. The program will then help you select which codes to activate. In many cases, a particular effect can be created through multiple methods. For example, to print bold characters, the printer might have three options:

1. Select a boldface code.
2. Print the line, backspace over the line, and then print it again.
3. Print the line, backspace over the line, move the printhead forward a few hundredths of an inch, and print the line again. This creates a thicker character than a simple overtype (and a simple overtype has no effect on a laser printer, which must use thicker lines to create a bold effect).

PFTSETUP will print several lines of samples, and ask you to select the number of the line that looks best (or to confirm the appearance of an effect). PFTSETUP will then apply the code used for the selected line to the actual code table used by PC Support. For the codes in this example exercise, the following line selections were used:

```
Superscript: 1
Underline: 1
Emphasis: 1
Backspace Test: Y
Mid-line pitch change: Y
Horizontal Character Spacing (5 pitch): Y
Horizontal Character Spacing (8.55 pitch): Y
Horizontal Character Spacing (10 pitch): Y
Horizontal Character Spacing (12 pitch): Y
Horizontal Character Spacing (15 pitch): Y
Horizontal Character Spacing (17.1 pitch): Y
PSM Test 1: 2
PSM Test 2: Y
Cursor Box Draw Characters: Y (Note: this may require
changes to the typeface settings to work properly,
depending on the front panel defaults for your
LaserJet).
Cursor Box Test 2: Y
```

After running through the confirmations, you can Esc to quit, and then select End and Save to apply the new settings. If there were problems with some of the tests (i.e., none of the selections looked right), then you may need to go back and check the codes that you entered. Something may have been mistyped.

You should now have a PFT that will work with PC Support. If you are using the DOS version of PC Support, the file will be in the right directory. However, if you are using the OS/2 version, you will need to copy the .PFT file to the \CMLIB directory. Furthermore, Communications Manager does not like the .PFT extension, so the file should be copied without an extension (e.g., COPY HPLASER2.PFT C:\CMLIB\HPLASER2).

At this point, you must tell PC Support to use the printer. Under OS/2 you go to the Communications Manager menu and select Advanced Configuration. Enter the name of the Configuration File. Now, select 5250 Workstation Feature Profiles. Select Printer Profiles, then Change, and enter the name of the printer profile. Unless you are using an unusual setup, the profile name will be 5250P1 (5250 Printer 1).

Select common printer options, and you will get an entry screen with several parameters. You can leave most settings as they are. The critical ones to check are printer type (select Printer Function Table) and host name (AS/400). When you leave this screen, Communications Manager will prompt for the printer function table name (HPLASER2, or whatever name you gave your customized table using PFTSETUP). You must also set a workstation ID—this is the name the AS/400 uses to identify the printer. This must be unique (you cannot duplicate the name of another printer connected to the AS/400). Generally, you should use a descriptive name (e.g., HPLJ_II_1 for Hewlett-Packard LaserJet Series II, number 1, then, if several LaserJets are connected, you can just change the last digit).

Now go to the Hardware Characteristics menu. The critical setting is: Prompt for Character Density = No. You should probably use Paper Handling = Continuous Forms, Number of Cut Sheet Drawers = 1 (unless you have multiple bin printer), Envelope Hopper = No (unless you have an envelope feeder), Paper Width = 8, and Font = Courier 10. If you select cut sheet paper handling instead of continuous forms, the WSF printer operator panel will prompt you for a new sheet for every page of the printout.

Set the serial/parallel ports to match the configuration on your PC. Make sure the initialization string is blank (all set to 0) since the initialization string was defined in the printer function table. If you have not previously done so, create a session assignment for the printer. Unless you have been changing your APPN definitions (not generally a good idea), the session settings should be:

5250 Workstation Function Profile Name: 5250P1
APPC Partner LU Alias: 5250PLU
APPC mode name: QPCSUPP

The short session ID must be unique among the 5250 sessions defined on your computer. For example, F for session 1, G for session 2, H for session 3, etc. This leaves letters A through E for terminal session names (the distinctive ranges for terminals and printers are not necessary, but can be convenient).

After setting all of the options, you must run verify to activate the profile. Then, you must shut down Communications Manager and restart it to use the new profile.

Appendix **B**

Beyond Automatic Configuration

Automatic configuration is very handy when first installing the system, but many people find it difficult to work around once the system is up and running. If you like to tweak the system and manually reconfigure attributes or follow a naming convention that does not lend itself to automatic configuration, you should turn automatic configuration off.

As an example, consider a printer that has been auto-configured to the wrong type. First log in as the QSYSOPR (or a user name with equivalent rights). Then follow the steps outlined below.

Turn off automatic configuration!

```
CHGSYSVAL
      SYSVAL(QAUTOCFG)
      VALUE('0')
```

Type WRKWTR (work with the writer) and selction option 4 next to the desired printer (e.g., PRT01) to stop the writer. Use WRKDEVD (work with device descriptions) option 8 (status) then option 2 (make unavailable).

Return to the main WRKDEVD screen and use option 3 to make a backup copy (e.g., PRT01BAK). Change the port and/or switch settings to an unused location. Leave all of the other parameters the same.

Use option 4 to delete the device (you may need to log on as QSECOFR or the equivalent to have delete authority).

Now use option 3 to copy the backup copy back under the original name (e.g., PRT01) and make the required device type changes on the parameter screen. You may want to make another backup copy of the new description. Then if you accidentally reactivate automatic configuration and destroy your new settings, a simple delete and copy will get you running again.

Select option 8 (work with status) and make the device available with option 1.

Return to WRKWTR and use option 1 to start the writer. You may want to select form type *STD rather than the default, *ALL, to keep the system from prompting the QSYSOPR for every new form type.

Index